DAVID A. GOLDENBERG

P9-CEI-197

POLITICAL ANTHROPOLOGY

By the same author

Ambiguous Africa: Cultures in Collision
Daily Life in the Kingdom of the Kongo: From
the Sixteenth to the Eighteenth Century

Georges Balandier

POLITICAL
ANTHROPOLOGY

Translated from the French by
A. M. Sheridan Smith

PANTHEON BOOKS
A Division of Random House, New York

Copyright © 1970 by Random House, Inc.

All rights reserved under International and Pan-American Copyright Conventions. Published in the United States by Pantheon Books, a division of Random House, Inc., New York, and simultaneously in Canada by Random House of Canada Limited, Toronto.

Originally published in France as "Anthropologie Politique" by Presses Universitaires de France. Copyright © 1967 by Presses Universitaires de France and in Great Britain by Allen Lane The Penguin Press.

Library of Congress Catalog Card Number: 69-20192
ISBN 0-394-44115-X

Manufactured in the United States of America

9 8 7 6 5 4 3 2

FIRST AMERICAN EDITION

Contents

Preface

This book is intended to satisfy a number of different needs. Its subject is *political anthropology*, a late specialization of social anthropology, whose theories, methods and results it attempts to present in a critical fashion. It proposes an initial synthesis and a general consideration of those political societies – alien to Western history – revealed by the anthropologists. These different aims involve, of course, certain risks – risks that are accepted in so far as all scientific knowledge is vulnerable and partially open to question. An undertaking of this kind could not have been envisaged without the progress already attained, during the past twenty years, by means of direct research, which has extended our knowledge of 'exotic' political systems, and of the most recent theoretical research. The Africanist anthropologists and sociologists have made an important contribution to this task, which explains the many references to their work.

This book is also intended to show how political anthropology is contributing to a clearer definition and a better knowledge of the political field. It defines a method of conducting field-work, and thus, at the same time, provides an answer to the criticism of certain specialists who reproach political anthropologists with directing their attention to an insufficiently defined object. It examines the relation of power to the elementary structures that form its primary basis, to the types of social stratification that make it necessary and to the rituals that link it to the sacred and influence its strategies. This approach could not ignore the problem of the state – and the characteristics of the traditional state are examined at length – but it shows how urgent it has become to dissociate political theory from the theory of the state. It shows that *all* human societies produce politics and that they are *all* subject to the vicissitudes of history. By that very fact, the concerns of political philosophy are rediscovered and, in a certain way, renewed.

This presentation of political anthropology has not excluded the statement of theoretical points of view. On the contrary, it has provided an opportunity of constructing a dynamic, critical anthropology in a particularly suitable field. In that sense, this book takes up, at a more general level, the preoccupations that emerged in the course of my research in Africa. It considers political societies not only from the point of view of the principles that govern their organization, but also in terms of the practices, strategies and manipulations they involve. It takes into account the gap that exists between the theories produced by societies and the approximate and vulnerable social reality that results from men's actions, from their politics. By the very nature of the object to which it is applied and by the problems it examines, political anthropology has acquired an unquestionable critical efficacy. In conclusion, it is worth recalling that this discipline now possesses a corrosive power, the effects of which are beginning to be felt by certain of the established theories. It contributes therefore to a renewal of sociological thought – a renewal necessitated as much by the force of circumstance as by the development of the social sciences.*

G. B.

*This work which uses the results of my own research carried out in the last ten years, owes much to remarks and suggestions made by the Groupe de Recherches en Anthropologie et Sociologie Politiques, of which I am director. Claudine Vidal and Francine Dreyfus, who are both members of this group, have given me particularly valuable help in the checking of evidence and in the revision of the manuscript.

Chapter One

The Construction
of Political Anthropology

Political anthropology appears both as a *project* – a very old, but ever-present one – and as a late *specialization* of anthropological research. In its first aspect it is an attempt to transcend particular political experiences and doctrines. It tends therefore to the establishment of a science of politics, regarding man as *homo politicus* and seeking properties common to all political organizations in all their historical and geographical diversity. In this sense, it is already present in Aristotle's *Politics*, which considers the human being as a naturally political being and attempts to discover laws, rather than lay down the best conceivable constitution for any possible state. In its second aspect, political anthropology is a subdivision of social anthropology or ethnology. It is concerned with the description and analysis of the political systems (structures, processes and representations) proper to societies regarded as primitive or archaic. In this sense, its existence as an independent discipline is of recent date. R. Lowie has contributed to its construction while deploring the inadequacy of anthropological work in the political field. One fact is significant: the meeting held in the United States in 1952, the International Symposium on Anthropology, scarcely gave it any attention at all. More recently still anthropologists continue to list its deficiencies: most of them admit that they have 'neglected the comparative study of political organization in primitive societies' (Schapera, 1956, p. 1). Hence the misunderstandings, errors and misleading statements that have led to the exclusion of political specialization and thought in the study of a great many societies.

In the last fifteen years this tendency has been reversed.

Field-work has increased, particularly in Black Africa, where over a hundred 'cases' have been observed and can be subjected to scientific treatment. Theoretical developments are beginning to emerge from the results acquired through this new research. This sudden progress may be explained as much by present-day events – the consideration of ex-colonial societies now in the process of transformation – as by the internal development of anthropological science. Political scientists now recognize the necessity of a political anthropology. G. Almond sees it as the prerequisite of any comparative political science. Raymond Aron states that the 'underdeveloped' societies 'are likely to fascinate political scientists who wish to escape from Western or industrial provincialism' (1965, pp. 1–2). And C. N. Parkinson remarks that 'some would conclude that the whole subject [the study of political theories] were better taken from the historian and handed to the social anthropologist' (1958, p. 11).

This latter-day success has been neither an unmixed nor an uncontested one. For certain philosophers, notably P. Ricoeur, political philosophy is justified *only* to the extent that the *political* is fundamentally the same from one society to another and *politics* is an 'aim' (*telos*) directed at the nature of the *polis*. This constitutes a total rejection of the sciences concerned with the political phenomenon; it can be refuted, in turn, only by a detailed examination of that phenomenon. The uncertainties that have for so long belaboured the respective fields, methods and aims of these disciplines are scarcely propitious for such an enterprise. An attempt must be made, however, to reduce these uncertainties.

1. The Significance of Political Anthropology

As a discipline aspiring to the status of a science, political anthropology is first of all a mode of recognition and knowledge of 'other', exotic political forms. It is an instrument for the discovery and study of the various institutions and practices that constitute the government of men, and the systems of thought and the symbols on which they are based. When Montesquieu develops the notion of *oriental despotism* (suggesting an ideal type in Max Weber's sense), places the societies thus defined in a class of their own and reveals political traditions different from those of Europe, he shows himself to be one of the earliest founders of political anthropology. Indeed, the place accorded to this model of political society in Marxist and neo-Marxist thought is proof of the importance of this contribution.

Montesquieu is, in fact, the initiator of a scientific enterprise that for a time performed the role of cultural and social anthropology. He draws up an inventory showing the diversity of human societies, based on ancient history, travellers' 'descriptions' and observations concerning foreign or strange countries. He sketches a method of comparison and classification, a typology; this leads him to give particular value to the political sphere and, in a way, identifies the types of society according to their modes of government. With a similar aim in view, anthropology first attempted to determine cultural areas and sequences on the basis of technico-economic criteria, the elements of civilization *and* the forms of the political structures.* Thus the 'political' becomes a relevant criterion for the differentiation of whole societies and civilizations: sometimes it is given a privileged scientific status. Political anthropology is seen as a discipline concerned with 'archaic' societies in which the state is not clearly constituted and societies in which the state exists and takes on a wide variety of forms. It must of course confront the problem of the state's origins and earliest forms: in devoting one of his principal works (*The Origin of the State*, 1927) to this question, Lowie returned to the same preoccupations as those of the pioneers of anthropological research. It is also

---

*J. H. Steward remarks in this connexion: 'The socio-political structure lends itself to classification and is more readily formulated than are other aspects of culture' (1966, p. 322 A).

confronted by the problem of segmentary societies, without a centralized political power, which are the object of an old, but ever-present debate. The historian F. J. Teggart, who is often quoted by British authors, states: 'Political organization is an exceptional thing, characteristic only of certain groups. . . . All peoples whatsoever have once been or still are organized on a different basis' (1918, p. 79). Thirty years later, the American sociologist R. MacIver continues to admit that 'tribal government differs from all other political forms' (1947, p. 158). Either by an essential difference or by the absence of the political, the societies relevant to anthropological study are in a class of their own. Simplistic dichotomies are proposed to explain this position: societies without political organization/ societies with political organization, without a state/with a state, without history or with a repetitive history/with a cumulative history, etc. These oppositions are very misleading; they create a false epistemological distinction, though the old distinction between primitive and civilized societies had a decisive influence at its inception. By postponing the methodical study of 'primitive systems of political organization', anthropologists have opened the way to negative interpretations by theoreticians, foreign to their discipline, who deny the existence of such systems.

These questions suggest the principal *aims* of political anthropology and continue to define it:

a. A determination of the political that links it neither to 'historical' societies alone, nor to the existence of a state apparatus.

b. An elucidation of the processes of the formation and transformation of political systems by means of research parallel with that of the historian; although the confusion of the 'primitive' and the 'first' is generally avoided, the examination of evidence relating to early times (to 'the true youth of the world', in Rousseau's phrase) or to periods of transition, is still accorded especial attention.

c. A comparative study, apprehending the different expressions of political reality, not within the limits of a particular history, that of Europe, but in its entire historical and geographical extension. In this sense, political anthropology wishes to become anthropology in the full sense of the term. It helps to reduce the 'provincialism' of the political scientists denounced by Aron and to construct 'the world history of political thought' desired by Parkinson.

The mutations that are taking place in the developing societies give an additional significance to the co-operative efforts of political anthropology and political sociology. They make possible the contemporary and non-retrospective study of the processes that govern the transition from tribal government and the traditional state to the modern state, from myth to political doctrine and ideology. It is a time particularly suited to such a study, one of those periods of profound change such as Saint-Simon saw in the industrial revolution, a period that sees the formation of a new type of society and civilization. The present situation of the 'exotic' political societies encourages one to examine, with due regard to the dynamic nature of the situation, the relations between traditional and modern political organizations, between tradition and modernism; moreover, in subjecting the first to a real test, it requires a new, more critical view of them. The confrontation goes beyond a study of the diversity and origin of political forms; it also poses the problem of their inter-relations in general, of their incompatibilities and antagonisms, their adaptations and their mutations.

2. The Development of Political Anthropology

Although political anthropology is primarily the consideration of political exoticism and the comparative analysis that results from it, its origins are very ancient indeed. Despite observations made in different periods, it developed only very slowly; there are reasons for its retarded development that partially explain its troubled history.

a. The precursors

When anthropologists reconstruct the itinerary of their science, they often rediscover the stepping-stones that provide evidence of the permanent (and inevitable) character of their basic preoccupations. Max Gluckman refers to Aristotle's 'treatise on government', his search for the causes of the decline of established governments and his attempt to determine the laws of political change. D. F. Pocock mentions the attention paid by Francis Bacon to evidence of different or 'savage' societies. Lloyd Fallers recalls that Machiavelli – in *The Prince* – distinguishes between two kinds of government, thus prefiguring two of the ideal types differentiated by Max Weber in his political sociology: 'patrimonialism' and 'sultanism'.

But the real initiators of the anthropological approach are to be found among the eighteenth-century creators of political thought. The most important precursor of all is still Montesquieu. Pocock emphasizes this fact in referring to *L'Esprit des Lois*: 'It is the first consistent attempt to survey the varieties of human society, to classify and compare them and, within society, to study the inter-functioning of institutions' (1961, p. 9). Because he defines societies according to their modes of government, Montesquieu lays the foundations of political sociology and anthropology. But there is more to be found in his work than a mere prefiguration, or the definition of a political form, 'oriental despotism', that was later to pass into scientific usage. According to L. Althusser, Montesquieu brought about 'a revolution in method'; he began with the facts, 'the laws, customs and various practices of the peoples of the earth'; he developed the notions of types and laws; he proposed a morphological and historical classification of societies – which, it is important to remember, are seen above all as political societies.

Of the early political philosophers, Rousseau – especially in his *Discours sur l'inégalité* and *Contrat social* – is the most often quoted. His contribution has not always been correctly evaluated by specialists in political sociology and anthropology. It cannot be reduced to the hypothetical contract by which mankind emerged from the 'primitive' state and changed its mode of existence, a theory that Parkinson dismisses as 'eighteenth-century rhetoric' and 'senility'. In pursuing the impossible search after origins, Rousseau considers scientifically the practices of 'savage peoples' and has an intuition of their historical and cultural dimensions. He adopts the relativism of *L'Esprit des Lois* and recognizes that the comparative study of societies makes for a better understanding of each of them. He develops an interpretation in terms of origins: inequality and the relations of production are the motive forces of history. He recognizes both the specificity and unbalance of all social systems – the permanent debate between the 'force of things' and the 'force of legislation'. The themes of the *Discours* sometimes prefigure Engels's analysis of 'the origin of the family, private property and the state'.

Indeed, a number of currents in eighteenth-century political thought are revived in the work of Marx and Engels. Their work contains the beginnings of an economic anthropology – with the discovery of an 'Asiatic mode of production' – and a political anthropology – notably with the reconsideration of 'oriental despotism' and its historical manifestations. They base their theories on various exotic documents: travellers' accounts and 'descriptions', writings on the village communities and the states of India in the nineteenth century and the works of historians and ethnographers. Their enterprise (it is an outline rather than finished work) has a dual aim: to discover the process of the formation of social classes and the state through the dissolution of the primitive communities and to determine the particular characteristics of an 'Asiatic' society. The approach involves a certain internal contradiction, particularly in Engels's contribution. Engels treats western history as representative of the general development of mankind, thus introducing a unitary view of the development of societies and cultures. Moreover, in so far as 'Asiatic' society and the state that governs it are regarded separately, it is in some way taken outside history and condemned to relative stagnation, to immutability. The same difficulty is to be found in all early anthropological research: on the one hand, it postulates the study of origins and processes of formation and transformation, while admitting that 'we do not consider that the origins of primitive institutions can be discovered' (Fortes and Evans-Pritchard); on the other hand, they concentrate on the most specific forms of societies and cultures, often to the detriment of an examination of the common characteristics and general processes that have contributed to their formation.

b. The first anthropologists

Political phenomena were considered by the early anthropologists above all from the point of view of origin – and with such obvious hesitation that one may well conclude that they had no real interest in that field. Gluckman denounces the complete inadequacy of their contribution to it: 'No early anthropologist, not even Maine, if we can claim him as an ancestor, had dealt with political problems, perhaps because all early research in anthropology was done on the small-scale societies of America, Australasia, Oceania, and India and its islands' (1963, p. 4).

However, there are frequent references to the pioneers. For example Sir Henry Maine, who was mentioned above and who is often neglected. His famous work *Ancient Law* (1861), a comparative study of Indo-European institutions, reveals the existence of two 'revolutions' in the development of societies: the change from societies based on status to societies based on contract; the change from social organizations centred on kinship to organizations governed by another principle – notably that of 'local contiguity', which defines 'the basis of common political action'. This double distinction lies at the origin of a debate that is still alive today. But the most frequently quoted reference is still *Ancient Society* (1877) by L. H. Morgan, the inspirer of Engels and the revered father of most modern anthropologists. He recognizes two 'fundamentally distinct' kinds of government significant of the early development of societies: 'The first, in the order of time, is founded upon persons, and upon relations purely personal, and may be distinguished as a society (*societas*). . . . The second is founded upon territory and upon property, and may be distinguished as a state (*civitas*). . . . Political society is organized upon territorial areas, and deals with property as well as with persons through territorial relations' (1877, pp. 6–7). This mode of interpretation practically leads anthropology to deprive a vast number of societies of politics. Morgan was the victim of his own theoretical system, which, in this case, was partly borrowed from Maine. He devoted several chapters of his great work to the 'idea of government', but he also denied the compatibility of the clan system (primitive society) with certain forms of organization that are essentially political (aristocracy, monarchy). He also revived a controversy that is constantly recurring in anthropological theory. In 1956, Schapera returned to it once again in his book *Government and Politics in Tribal Societies*.

c. The political anthropologists

It was not until after 1920 that a differentiated political anthropology, explicit and not implicit, was developed. It set out to study old problems, but it used new material provided by ethnographical research. It revived discussion of the state, its origin and primitive manifestations – a question that had already been treated by Franz Oppenheimer in the early years of the century (*Der Staat*, 1907).

Within a few years of each other two important studies, showing the same preoccupation, were published: *The Origin of the State Reconsidered in the Light of the Data of Aboriginal North America* (1924) by W. C. MacLeod, who uses evidence accumulated by American ethnographers, and *The Origin of the State* (1927) by R. H. Lowie, who determines the respective roles of internal factors (those responsible for social differentiation) and of external factors (those resulting from conquest) in the formation of states. Both works were the result of approaches that wished to be scientific, based on facts, and sharply distinct from the intentions of political philosophy. The problem of origins was also considered by Sir James Frazer, who examined the relations between magic, religion and kingship and who became the initiator of the study of the relation between power and the sacred. New fields of research were opened up. Some of these led to the recognition and interpretation of exotic theories of government. In 1927, Beni Prasad published his *Theory of Government in India.** General works by political scientists began to make brief incursions into anthropology; thus the *History of Political Theories* (1924) by A. A. Goldenweiser referred particularly to the political system of the Iroquois of North America.

The first anthropological treatises paid little attention to political factors; Franz Boas devoted a chapter of his *General Anthropology* to the problems of government, while *Primitive Society* by Lowie systematized the author's theses and contributed a brief account of the principal results. But the crucial anthropological revolution took place in the 1930s, a period that saw a great increase in field-work and, accordingly, of theoretical or methodological developments. The research devoted to segmentary societies (the so-called stateless societies), to the structures of kinship and to the models of relationships

---

*During the 1920s there was a great increase in the number of studies devoted to Hindu political thought; particularly worthy of mention are those of U. Ghostal (1923), Ajiir Kumar Sen (1926) and N. C. Bandyopadhaya (1927).

that regulate these structures, led to a better definition of the political field and a better understanding of its diversity.

It was in the field of African studies that the most rapid progress was accomplished. The societies investigated were organized on a larger scale; the differentiation of the relations of kinship and strictly political relations was expressed more clearly in the 'archaic' micro-societies. In 1940, three works were published that have since acquired classical status. Two of these, by E. E. Evans-Pritchard, contained the results of direct research and had new theoretical implications. *The Nuer*, a book that presents the general features of a Nilotic society, also reveals the relations and political institutions of a people apparently without government; it shows that an 'ordered anarchy' can exist. *The Political System of the Anuak* is exclusively a study in political anthropology and concerns a Sudanese people – neighbours of the Nuer – who have developed two contrasting and concurrent forms of human government. The third work, *African Political Systems*, is a collection of essays edited by Evans-Pritchard and Meyer Fortes. By presenting a number of clearly differentiated 'cases', it has great value as a comparative study; it is preceded by a theoretical introduction and offers the outline of a typology. Gluckman regards it as the first contribution in an attempt to give scientific status to political anthropology. It is true that the editors of the book are anxious to dissociate themselves from 'political philosophers' who are concerned not so much to 'describe' as to 'state what form of government mankind *ought* to have'. This view has been met, of course, with a good deal of disagreement, but there is scarcely a specialist who does not reveal his debt to these two great anthropologists.

Since 1945 there has been a rapid increase in the number of specialists in the fields of African politics. Their studies are primarily the result of intensive field-work. They examine both segmentary societies (Fortes, Middleton and Tait, Southall, Balandier) and state societies (Nadel, Smith, Maquet, Mercier,

Apter, Beattie). They attempt to provide a theoretical framework and regional syntheses based on related systems. *Tribes without Rulers*, published in 1958 under the editorship of Middleton and Tait, deals with lineage-dominated societies. *Primitive Government*, by Lucy Mair, published in 1962, concerns the states of the eastern interlacustrian region. Schapera's *Government and Politics in Tribal Societies* (1956) has, as its title suggests, a more general scope, though it is based entirely on examples from southern Africa. It examines the mechanisms by which primitive governments function and elucidates certain problems of terminology. More recent research has been affected by situations following independence and forms a link between political anthropology and political science (Apter, Coleman, Hodgkin, Potekhin, Ziegler). They show the necessity for interdisciplinary cooperation.

Outside the Africanist field, a single work dominates the specialized literature, Edmund Leach's *Political Systems of Highland Burma* (1954), which is devoted to the political structures and organizations of the Kachin of Burma. This study gives particular prominence to the political aspect of social phenomena. Following Nadel (and his predecessors), the society as a whole and the 'political unit' are identified, while the social structures are themselves examined from the point of view of 'ideas concerning the distribution of power between persons and groups of persons'. Leach develops – and this is his major contribution – a dynamic structuralism, with a wealth of suggestions most useful for political anthropology. He shows the relative instability of socio-political equilibriums (they are 'moving equilibriums', in Pareto's phrase), the effects of contradictions, the gap between the system of social and political relations and the system of ideas associated with them. We must now turn to a more thorough examination of questions of method.

3. Methods and Tendencies in Political Anthropology

At the outset the methods used were no different from those of anthropology generally. They became more specific when a still implicit political anthropology confronted what were to become its own peculiar problems: the formative process of state societies, the nature of the primitive state, the forms of political power in societies with minimal government, etc. They acquired their full originality when political anthropology became a scientific project with a properly determined object and aims. They then came under the influence of the established political sociologies – that of Max Weber, or, less frequently, that of Marx and Engels (as in the case of Leslie White). But they also benefited from the progress of anthropology generally.

These methods are characterized by the instruments they use and by the problems to which they are applied. They are inadequately defined by contrasting theoretical work, which constructs its area of study on the basis of field-work, and the work that confines itself to the immediate development of the data derived from direct research. Before evaluating their scientific efficacy in the recognition of the political field, a brief account of these methods should be drawn up.

a. The genetic approach

This is both the earliest method in the history of the discipline and the most ambitious. It concerns the problems of origin and long-term 'evolution': the magical and/or religious origin of kingship, the process of the formation of the primitive state, the transition from societies based on kinship to political societies, etc. It is illustrated by a series of works – from those of the pioneers to W. C. MacLeod's historical study *The Origin and History of Politics* (1931). In a way, it culminates in the ethnological research which, inspired by Marxism, links it to a dialectical conception of the history of societies.

b. The functionalist approach

It identifies the political institutions of 'primitive' societies on the basis of function. In Radcliffe-Brown's view it leads to an examination of 'political organization' as an *aspect* of 'the total organization of society'. In fact, the analysis reveals properly political institutions (the apparatus of kingship, for example) and multifunctional institutions, which, in certain circumstances, are used for political purposes (e.g. the 'alliances' established between the clans and lineages). This type of approach makes it possible to define political relations, and the organizations and systems on which they are based, but it has contributed little to the elucidation of the *nature* of the political phenomenon. This is generally characterized by two groups of functions: those that establish or maintain the social order by assuring internal cooperation (Radcliffe-Brown) and those that guarantee security by defending the political unit.

c. The typological approach

This is an extension of the functionalist approach. It attempts to determine *types* of systems, to classify the forms of political organization. The existence or non-existence of the primitive state seems to provide an initial criterion of differentiation: this is the principal approach of *African Political Systems*. This dichotomic interpretation is now open to question. In fact, it is impossible to construct a series of types ranging from systems with minimal government to systems with a clearly formed state. In progressing from one type to others, political power becomes more differentiated, more complex and more centralized. The simple opposition of *segmentary societies* and *centralized state societies* became even more questionable when the Africanist A. Southall showed the need to introduce at least one further category, that of *segmentary states*.

But quite apart from this criticism the method itself is now in doubt, to such an extent indeed that typology is seen as little more than a useless 'tautology' (Leach). It is important, to say the least, to distinguish between 'descriptive' and 'deductive' typologies (D. Easton). It is also important not to avoid the major difficulty: the types are 'fixed', and, as Leach put it so forcefully, 'we can no longer be satisfied with attempts to establish a typology of fixed systems'.

d. The terminological approach

An initial examination and classification of political phenomena and systems leads inevitably to an attempt to construct basic categories. This is a difficult task that requires, in the first place, a precise delimitation of the political field.* It is a task that is far from complete: in an essay on political anthropology, the political scientist D. Easton affirms that the object of this discipline is still ill defined, because 'numerous conceptual problems have not been resolved'. One of the most advanced attempts along these lines is that of M. G. Smith; he tries to establish the basic notions: political action, competition, power, authority, administration, office, etc.; it is especially useful, in its results, in that it examines 'political action' in an analytical manner, in ord er to discover the elements common to all systems. But it is easier to draw up a vocabulary of key concepts than to give them real content.

The development of these concepts must be completed by a systematic study of indigenous political categories and theories, whether they are explicit or implicit, and however difficult their translation may be. Linguistics therefore is an indispensable instrument for political anthropology and sociology. One cannot ignore the fact that the societies concerned by the first of these disciplines require an elucidation of the theories that explain them and the ideologies that justify them. A. Southall, John

*Cf. Chapter 2, 'The Political Sphere'.

Beattie and Georges Balandier have suggested the means to be used in constructing systems that express indigenous political thought.

e. The structuralist approach

This approach replaces the genetic or functionalist study by a study of politics on the basis of structural models. The political is seen in terms of *formal* relations that express the real power relations between individuals and groups. At its simplest this interpretation sees political structures – and all social structures – as abstract systems that express the principles that unite the elements that make up concrete political societies. In a stimulating article on 'the power structure of the Hajerai' (Pouillon, 1964), a group of Chad peoples, J. Pouillon suggests and illustrates one of the possibilities of the structuralist method applied to the field of political anthropology. It is applied to a group of micro-societies that possess both kinship relations (the general name Hajerai suggests this) and significant variations, notably in the treatment of 'power'. A double condition, the presence of common elements and differentiation in the arrangement of them, is necessary to this approach; it makes it possible, in two stages, to construct 'systems' corresponding to the totality of the modalities of socio-political organization *and* a 'system of systems', whose purpose is to define Hajerai power. Hence the two stages of the study, the first being the discovery of 'the internal structural relations of each organization considered as a system' and the second the interpretation of the organizations studied, as a totality, 'as if it were the product of a combinative'. In the case under examination the method particularly brings out the different combinations (equivalence, partial differentiation, variable accentuation) of the religious and political powers, the play of logic expressed in various forms within the same overall structure.

When applied to the study of political systems the structuralist approach raises difficulties that are peculiar to it at a more general level – in particular those considered by Leach, a moderate structuralist, in his study of Kachin political society. He sets out with the obvious fact that the structures developed by the anthropologist are models that exist only as 'logical constructions'. This fact involves an initial question: how can one be certain that the formal model is the most adequate? Later, Leach examines a more essential difficulty. 'Structural systems as described by anthropologists are always static systems'; they are models of social reality that present a state of coherence and accentuated balance, whereas this reality does not possess the character of a coherent whole; it contains contradictions, it manifests variations *and* modifications of structure. In the particular case of Kachin political organization, Leach discovers the phenomenon of oscillation between two poles, the 'democratic' type (*gumlao*) and the 'aristocratic' (*shan*), the instability of the system and the variable adjustments of the culture, the socio-political structure and the ecological environment. The rigour of several of the structural analyses is misleading and more apparent than real. It is explained by a necessary, but often concealed condition: 'The description of certain unreal types of situation – namely the structure of equilibrium systems' (Leach).

f. The dynamist approach

This approach completes, in a sense, the preceding one, correcting it on certain points. It attempts to seize the dynamic of the structures as well as the system of relations that form it: that is, to take into account the incompatibilities, the contradictions, the tensions *and* the movement inherent in any society. This is particularly necessary in political anthropology because it is in the political sphere that such factors are most apparent and that history most clearly leaves its mark.

Leach contributed directly to the development of this

approach, while seeking the reasons for its late appearance. He questions the dominant influence of Durkheim – to the detriment of that of Pareto or Weber – which made possible a conception that stressed structural equilibriums, cultural uniformities and forms of solidarity – to such an extent that societies with obvious internal conflicts or those open to change were 'suspected of anomy'. He condemned the 'academic prejudices' and ethnocentrism of anthropologists who eliminated certain data in order to deal only with societies that were stable, free from internal contradictions and isolated within their frontiers. In short, Leach forces us to consider the contradictory, the conflicting, the approximative and the *external* relational. This development is proving necessary to the progress of political anthropology, for politics is primarily about competition and the confrontation of interests.

The anthropologists of the Manchester school, led by Max Gluckman, direct their research according to a dynamic interpretation of societies. Gluckman has examined the nature of the relations between 'customs' and 'conflict' (*Custom and Conflict in Africa*, 1955), 'order' and 'rebellion' (*Order and Rebellion in Tribal Africa*, 1963). His contribution concerns both the general theory of traditional, archaic societies and the method of political anthropology. Suggestions for the second are to be found in his theory of rebellion and in his studies of certain African states. Rebellion is seen as a permanent process that constantly affects political relations, while ritual is seen as a means of expressing conflicts and, at the same time, of transcending them by affirming the unity of the society. The traditional African state seems to be unstable and the bearer of organized – ritualized – contestation that does more to maintain the system than to change it; relative instability and controlled rebellion are thus the normal manifestation of the political processes proper to this kind of state. The theoretical innovation is obviously a real one, but it is not carried to its logical conclusion. Gluckman certainly recognizes the internal dynamic as *constitutive* of any society, but he reduces its power to change things. It is taken into account – as are the effects resulting from 'external conditions' – but it operates within a view of history that links the societies studied by anthropology to a history that is regarded as *repetitive*.

This interpretation gives rise to a debate that cannot be ignored; its importance is expressed in the growing interest in historically minded anthropological analyses and the increase in the number of theoretical essays that evaluate it. After a long period of disfavour, due to the excessive ambitions of the evolutionist school, the naïveties of the diffusionist school and the negative bias of the functionalist school, these questions are re-emerging as of primary importance in the field of anthropological research. A small work by Evans-Pritchard (*Anthropology and History*, 1961) contributes to this rehabilitation of history. This debate will be resolved only if a clear distinction is made between the means of historical knowledge, the forms taken by historical development and the ideological expressions with which real history is clothed. The elucidation of the relations between these three registers is a necessary condition for the development of political anthropology.

In a field that has been regarded for so long as being outside history – that of African Negro societies and cultures – recent work has begun to show the falseness of over-static interpretations. The reality of African history, as expressed in its effects on the life and death of these political societies and cultures cannot be ignored. Taking such factors into account research has shown that historical consciousness did not appear by accident, as a result of colonization and modern transformations. It shows – and in doing so weakens the point of view of Jean-Paul Sartre – that it was not only foreign history that was 'interiorized'. In his study of the Nupe (Nigeria), S. F. Nadel distinguishes two levels of historical expression (that of ideological history and that of objective history) and declares that the Nupe possess a historical consciousness (he specifically calls them 'historically minded') that operates on each of these two registers.* New research has confirmed this duality of historical expression and the knowledge that controls it: a *public* history (unchanging in its general features and concerning a whole ethnic entity) coexists with a *private* history (defined in detail, subject to distortions, concerned with particular groups, and their specific interests). A study by Ian Cunnison of the people of Luapula, in Central Africa, provides a concrete illustration. It defines the respective situation of these two modalities of African history: at the impersonal level of history, time and change are linked; at the 'personal' level, time is abolished and changes are regarded as unimportant – the positions and interests of groups are *fixed* in some way. Moreover, this analysis shows to what an extent the 'Luapula' are aware of the role of events in the development of their society and have acquired a sense of historical causality; for them, this causality does not belong to the supernatural order, for events are subject mainly to man's will.

The link between history and politics is obvious, even in the case of societies that come within the anthropological sphere. As soon as these societies are no longer seen as fixed systems, the essential relation between their social dynamic and their history can no longer be ignored. But there is another, even more powerful reason: the degrees of historical consciousness are in correlation with the forms and degree of the centralization of the political power. In segmentary societies, the sole guardians of knowledge of the past are usually the holders of power. In state societies, historical consciousness seems to be more vital and more widespread. Moreover, it is in such state societies that the use of ideological history for strategic political ends is most clearly seen at work; J. Vansina has shown this very well in the case of traditional Rwanda. Lastly, it should be remembered that the progress of the colonial countries towards independence has provided the various nationalisms with a rich history of militancy. It can be seen, therefore, that the dynamic theory of societies, political anthropology, political sociology and history

*Cf. *A Black Byzantium*, Oxford University Press, 1942.

have been forced to join forces. And this conjunction gives new emphasis to Durkheim's prediction: 'We are convinced . . . that the day will come when the historical spirit and the sociological spirit will differ only in detail.'

Chapter Two

The Political Sphere

From the outset political anthropology was faced with the debates that were so essential to the existence of political philosophy. Indeed, these debates placed political philosophy in such danger that R. Polin, among others, showed the urgent need to present a modern 'definition' and 'defence' of them. At their most ambitious, both disciplines strive to discover the essential nature of politics in the diversity of the forms in which it is expressed. But there seems to be a certain ambiguity about their relations. The first anthropologists condemned the ethnocentrism of most political theories: Lowie sees them as centred primarily on the state and as using a unilateral conception of the government of human societies. In this sense, political philosophy is identified with a philosophy of the state and scarcely conforms with the data resulting from the study of 'primitive' societies. Modern anthropologists contrast the scientific nature of their research with the normative character of political philosophy, the validity of their results with the unproved conclusions of the theoreticians. These criticisms may not have been enough to give political anthropology a less vulnerable basis, but they served the cause of such radical political scientists as Parkinson, who wishes to draw his colleagues 'off the beaten tracks' and urges them to build up 'a world history of political thought'. His plea is reminiscent in a way of the desire of specialists to make political anthropology a true comparative science of government. But this common desire for 'objective' knowledge and a de-occidentalization of data does not eliminate the initial considerations of any political philosophy. How is politics to be identified and qualified? How is it to be 'built up' if it is not an obvious expression of social reality? How are its specific functions to be determined if one admits – as do several anthropologists – that certain primitive societies have no political organization?

1. Maximalists and Minimalists

Ethnographical information, which is based on direct research, reveals a great diversity of primitive political forms, whether in the American field – from Eskimo bands to the imperial state of the Incas of Peru – or the African field – from the bands of Pygmies and Negrilloes to the traditional states, some of which, such as the Mossi Empire and the Ganda kingdom, still survive. This variety calls for classifications and typologies, but above all it necessitates the preliminary question of the definition and delimitation of the political field. The specialists are divided into two camps on this matter, with maximalists on the one hand and minimalists on the other. The maximalists, who invoke old and still revered sources, might take as their motto Bonald's opinion that there is no society without government. In the *Politics* Aristotle sees man as a 'naturally' political being and identifies the state with the social group which, because it embraces all the others and transcends them in power, can in fact exist of its own accord. When carried to its logical conclusion, this mode of interpretation leads to a total identification of the political unit with the society as a whole. Thus, in his study of the bases of social anthropology, Nadel writes: 'When one examines a society, one finds the political unit, and when one speaks of the former, one is in fact considering the latter; so much so that it is the political institutions that control and maintain the widest corporate group, that is, the society' (1961, p. 141). Leach accepts this identification, and implicitly the equality set up between the society and the political unit defined by its capacity of maximum inclusiveness.

Some functionalist analyses do not contradict this wide use of the term politics. When Schapera defines political organization as the aspect of total organization that ensures the establishment and maintenance of 'internal co-operation and external independence' he links, through the second of these functions, his idea of politics to those previously mentioned.

The minimalists prove negative or ambiguous in their attitude towards the theory that all primitive societies possess governments. They include a great many historians and sociologists, a notable exception being Max Weber, who pointed out that politics preceded the state, which, far from being the same thing as politics, was merely one of its historical manifestations. Similarly, anthropologists, early and modern, are among those who question the universality of political phenomena. One of the 'founders', W. C. MacLeod sees the peoples that he considers – such as the Yurok of California – as being without political organization and as living in a state of anarchy (*The Origin and History of Politics*, 1931). Bronislaw Malinowski maintains that 'political groups are absent' from the Vedda and Australian aborigines and Robert Redfield emphasizes that political institutions may be entirely absent from 'the most primitive' societies. And even Radcliffe-Brown, in his study of the Andamanese (*The Andaman Islanders*, 1922), recognizes that these islanders possess no 'organized government'.

In fact, such denials of political life are seldom absolute in character; they usually express the lack of institutions comparable with those of the modern state. Because of this implicit ethnocentrism, they cannot be satisfactory. Hence the attempts that aim at breaking down the oversimplified dichotomy that separates tribal societies and those with clearly constituted, rational government. These attempts operate in different ways. They may characterize the political sphere not so much by its modes of organization as by the functions performed – in which case it becomes a concept of wider application. They also tend to mark out a *threshold* from which politics is clearly apparent. Lucy Mair remarks: 'Some anthropologists would hold that the sphere of politics begins where that of kinship ends' (1962, p. 10). Otherwise the difficulty is met head on and knowledge of the political fact is sought among societies in which it is least apparent – the 'segmentary' societies. M. G. Smith (1956), for example, devotes a long article to the lineage societies, which he sees from three points of view: as a system possessing formal characteristics, as a mode of relationship quite distinct from kinship and above all as a structure with political content. He is led to regard political life as an *aspect* of all social life, not as the product of specific units or structures, and to reject as irrelevant the rigid distinction between 'State societies' and 'stateless societies'. But this interpretation is also contested, notably by Easton, in an article on the problems of political anthropology: in his opinion Smith's theoretical analysis operates at such an elevated level that it is unable to grasp in what ways political systems resemble each other, because it fails to examine in what ways they differ. As a result we are left in as much uncertainty as ever.

2. Confrontation of Methods

The ambiguity is to be found in the facts, the methods and the technical vocabulary of the specialists. The Greek word *polis* provides the common root for at least three distinct notions in the English language – 'polity', 'policy' and 'politics'. Obviously, a clear distinction must be drawn between:

1. the modes of government of human societies;
2. the types of action employed in the management of public affairs;
3. the strategies resulting from the competition of individuals and groups.

A fourth category should also be added, that of political knowledge; it is important to consider the means of interpretation and justification employed in the political life of a society. These various aspects are not always differentiated, nor treated equally. When emphasis is placed on one or other of them, different definitions of the political sphere emerge.

a. Definition by modes of spatial organization

Henry Maine and Lewis Morgan gave particular importance to the territorial criterion. In the first instance, the political sphere is seen as a system of organization operating within the framework of a clearly marked territory, a political unit or a space occupied by a political community. This criterion appears in most definitions of political organization (in the wide sense) and of the state. Max Weber characterizes political activity, apart from the legitimate use of force, by the fact that it takes place within a territory with definite frontiers; it establishes a clear separation between the 'interior' and the 'exterior' and has a significant influence over behaviour. Radcliffe-Brown also accepts the territorial framework among the elements that define political organization. Other later anthropologists do the same, including Schapera, who has shown that the simplest societies achieve internal cohesion on the basis both of kinship *and* territory. Indeed, this recalls Lowie's belief in the compatibility of the kinship principle and the territorial principle.

In a single case study – that of the segmentary society of the Nuer of Sudan – Evans-Pritchard lays emphasis on the determination of the political field by reference to territorial organization. 'Between local groups,' he says, 'there are relations of a structural order that can be called political ... The territorial system of the Nuer is always the dominant variable in its relation to the other social systems' (1940, p. 265).

There is then a wide measure of agreement. F. X. Sutton is led to formulate a question of method (1959). Do territorial representations lie at the heart of political systems? If so, the study of them would become the first approach of political anthropology and sociology, while recourse to the notions of power and authority remains contestable to the extent that every social structure produces them.

b. Definition by function

Apart from this determination by the territory on which it operates and which it organizes, the political is frequently defined by the functions it performs. In their more general form, these functions are seen as ensuring internal cooperation and the defence of the society's integrity against external threat. They contribute to the 'physical survival' of society, to use Nadel's words, and make possible the regulation or resolution of conflicts. To these functions of conservation are usually added those of decision and the direction of public affairs, even if, in the formal aspects of government, they are of a different kind.

Certain recent theoretical studies carry the functionalist analysis further. An example of this is G. A. Almond's Introduction to the collective work, *The Politics of Developing Areas* (1960). Almond defines the political system as carrying out, in every independent society 'the functions of integration and adaptation' by recourse to, or by the threat of recourse to, the legitimate use of physical constraint. This wide interpretation makes it possible not to confine the political sphere to specialized organizations and structures; it aims at the formulation of categories that are applicable to all societies and, on this basis, the development of a comparative political science.

Among the characteristics common to all political systems, Almond draws particular attention to two: the performing of the same functions by all political systems and the multifunctional aspect of all political structures – none of them being completely specialized. The comparison may be made if one bears in mind the degree of specialization and the means used to perform the 'political functions'. What are these functions? Their identification is made all the more necessary in that a comparative study cannot be confined to an examination of structures and organizations alone; if it were, it would be as inadequate as 'a comparative anatomy without a comparative physiology'. Almond distinguishes two broad categories of functions: the first concerns politics as *lato sensu* – the 'social-ization' of individuals and the training of them for political 'roles', the confrontation and adjustment of 'interests', the communication of symbols and 'messages'; the second con-cerns government – the formulation and application of 'rules'. Such a division of functions enables us to return to the various aspects of the political field, but at a level of generalization that facilitates comparison by reducing the gap between developed political societies and 'primitive' political societies.

The functional interpretation ignores certain basic questions. It takes insufficient account of the dynamisms that ensure the cohesion of society as a whole, such as those referred to by Gluckman when he observes that this cohesion depends on the division of society into a series of opposed groups involving over-lapping membership, or when he interprets certain forms of 'rebellion' as contributing to the maintenance of the social order. Moreover, it remains imprecise in certain ways for political functions are not the only ones to preserve this order. Radcliffe-Brown characterizes them by their use, or possible use, of physi-cal force. He echoes the theories of Hobbes and of Weber, for whom force is the means used by politics, the *ultima ratio*, *domination* (*Herrschaft*) being at the heart of politics.

It is through coercion – legitimately used – that political functions and structures are usually qualified. But it is more a concept of delimitation than a concept of definition; it does not completely describe the political field, any more than the criter-ion of currency completely covers the field of economics.

c. Definition by the modalities of political action

Most recent studies by younger anthropologists have shifted their analysis from the functions to the *aspects* of political action. After remarking on the confusions of the technical voca-bulary and the inadequacies of the methodology, M. G. Smith suggests a new formulation of the problems. For him, political life is an aspect of social life: 'A political system is simply a system of political action.' But if the formula is not to be reduced to a mere tautology, the content of this political action must be determined. Social action is political when it seeks to control or influence *decisions* concerning public affairs, that is, *policy*. The content of these decisions varies according to the cultural contexts and the social units within which they are expressed, but the processes of which they are the culmination always operate within the framework of the competition between individuals and groups. All social units concerned with this competition have, by this very fact, a political character.

Smith also contrasts political action and administrative action, despite their close association in the government of human societies. Political action takes place at the level of decision and of more or less explicitly formulated 'programmes', administrative action at the level of organization and execution. The first is defined by power, the second by authority. Smith goes on to say that political action is of its nature 'segmentary', since it is expressed in the interplay of groups and persons in competition. On the other hand, administrative action is of its nature 'hierarchical', for it organizes, to varying degrees and according to strict rules, the direction of public affairs. The government of a society always, and everywhere, implies this double form of action. Consequently, political systems are distinguished only to the extent in which they vary in the degree of differentiation and the mode of association of these two kinds of action. Their typology should not therefore be discontinuous, like that of contrasting segmentary and centralized state societies, but form a series of types in which political action and administrative action are combined in different degrees.*

Easton formulates a double criticism of this analytical approach: it invokes a 'postulate' (the existence of hierarchic-administrative relations in the lineage systems) and it conceals the 'significant differences' between the various political

*Cf. the theoretical contributions of M. G. Smith (1956), and the general chapters of *Government in Zazzau* (Smith, 1960).

systems. Nevertheless, he places his own approach in a similar context. Action may be said to be political 'when it is more or less directly related to the formulation and execution of binding or authoritative decisions for a social system' (Easton, 1959, p. 226). From this point of view political decisions are taken within very diverse social units, such as families, kinship groups, lineages, associations and enterprises, some of whose activities constitute, in a sense, the 'political system' itself. This loose interpretation is devoid of scientific efficacity. Indeed, Easton is obliged to confine the idea of system to 'those activities more or less directly related to the making of binding decisions for a society and its major subdivisions' (1959, p. 227). He defines the political, then, by a certain form of social action, the form which ensures the taking and carrying out of decisions, and by a field of application, 'the most inclusive social system', that is, society as a whole. Easton then considers the conditions required for political decision-making to operate: the formulation of demands and the reduction of their contradictions, the existence of a body of custom or legislation, the administrative means of carrying out the decisions, the organisms responsible for taking the decisions and the instruments for 'supporting' the state power. On the basis of these initial data, he distinguishes between the 'primitive' political systems and 'modern' systems. In the first case, the 'support structures' are variable, the established regime is seldom threatened by the conflicts that often emerge in new political communities. This approach, then, emphasizes the specifically anthropological data, at the expense of reintroducing implicitly the dichotomy that it claims to be eliminating.

d. Definition by formal characteristics

Each of the previous attempts tries to discover the more general aspects of the political field, either by means of the frontiers that enclose it in space, or the functions or modes of action in which it is expressed. It is now recognized that the comparative method, which justifies anthropological research, creates a dependence on abstract units and processes rather than on real units and processes: both Nadel and Gluckman agree on this point.

The work of the 'structuralists', which operates at a high level of abstraction and formalization, scarcely concerns the system of political relations – for reasons that are not entirely accidental. In fact, it provides structures, which it then 'fixes' – with a consequent loss of dynamism, as Leach has already remarked – from a monist point of view. This explains why they cannot be easily adapted to the study of the political sphere, where competition breeds pluralism, where the equilibriums are always vulnerable and where power creates a field of forces. If, like Leach, one distinguishes between the 'system of ideas' and the 'real' political system, it must be admitted that the structuralist method is better suited to an analysis of the first than of the second. It must also be noted that 'the ideal structure of society', despite the fact that it is 'both elaborate and rigid', is made up of categories whose fundamental ambiguity makes it possible to interpret social (and political) life as always being in conformity with the formal model. As a result it introduces significant distortions.

An analysis by Pouillon, presented as part of a group study devoted to political anthopology,* illustrates the structuralist approach to this discipline. It seeks first of all a definition of the political: is it a sphere of facts or an aspect of social phenomena? In classical anthropological literature, the answer was based on the notions of the unified society (political unit), the state (present or absent), power and subordination (the bases of the social order). Pouillon considers such notions to be inadequate and remarks that all subordination is not necessarily political, that all societies and all groups do not possess a single order, but more or less compatible *orders*, and, finally, that in case of

* Groupe de Recherches en Anthropologie et Sociologie Politiques (Sorbonne et École Pratique des Hautes Études).

conflict, one order must predominate over the others. According to Pouillon, this last point determines the definition of the political: he points out that in a unified society one structure *pre-dominates* over the others. This predominant structure varies according to the societies, according to their characteristics of territorial size, number and way of life.

This leads to another formulation of the questions proper to political anthropology: what are the 'circuits' that explain why certain men can command others? How is the relation of command and obedience established? Stateless societies are those in which power lies in pre-political circuits – those created by kinship, religion and economics. Statist societies are those that possess specialized circuits; however, these new circuits do not abolish the pre-existing circuits, which survive and provide them with a formal model. Thus, the structure of kinship, even if fictitious or forgotten, may shape the traditional state. From this point of view, one of the tasks of political anthropology is to discover the conditions in which these specialized conditions appear.

A shift has been made, then, from the order of structures to the order of origins. This is explained by the transition, in the course of the debate, from the field of formal relations (from the order of orders) to that of real relations (of command and domination). Moreover, and this difficulty seems to be a fundamental one, to affirm that the structure that is imposed as a last resort is political is to beg the question.

e. Evaluation

This summary of the various approaches to the subject also serves as a summary of the difficulties confronting anthropologists when they turn to the political sphere. It shows that the boundaries are still imprecise and questionable, that each School has its own way of drawing them, while often using the same instruments. This uncertainty is greatest in the societies with 'minimal government' and 'diffused government' (Lucy Mair); the same partners and the same groups may have many different functions – varying according to the situation, as in a play performed by a single actor. Political aims are not always attained by means of 'political' relations and, inversely, these relations may satisfy interests of a quite different nature. J. Van Velsen, in a work devoted to the Tonga of East Africa, and Clyde Mitchell in his preface to the same book state the problem at another level of generalization: 'Social relationships are more instrumental in the activities of people than they are the determinants of them' (Van Velsen, 1964, p. x). He goes on to define a method that he calls 'situational analysis'; such a new means of study is necessary, he believes, because 'norms, general rules of conduct, are translated into practice, that is, they are ultimately manipulated by individuals in particular situations to serve particular ends' (p. xxiv). In the case of the Tonga, for whom power is linked neither to structural positions nor to specific groups, political behaviour is expressed only in certain situations. And these situations occur within an 'ever-fluctuating network of links and cross-linkages'.

The frontiers of the political must not be traced only in relation to the various orders of social relations, but also in relation to the *culture*, either as a whole or in certain of its elements. In his study of Kachin society (Burma), Leach has revealed an overall correlation between the two systems: the less cultural integration is developed, the more political integration is effective, at least through submission to a single mode of political action. Similarly, he has shown myth and ritual to be a 'language' that provides the arguments for justifying claims to rights, status and power. In fact, myth contains an element of ideology; it is, in Malinowski's words, a 'social charter' that ensures 'the existing form of society with its system of distributing power, privilege and property'; it has a justificatory function that the guardians of tradition and the controllers of the political apparatus know how to exploit. It belongs, then, to the field of political anthropology, in the same way as ritual, in certain of its manifestations – when, for example, the rituals are exclusively (in the case of cults and procedures concerning kingship) or inclusively (in the case of ancestor worship) the sacred instruments of power.

The difficulties of identifying the political are also to be found at the economic level, if one considers separately the very *apparent* connexion between the relations of production governing social stratification and the relations of power. Certain economic privileges (land rights, labour levies, market rights, etc.) and certain economic obligations (of generosity and assistance) are associated with the exercise of power and authority. There are also economic confrontations, of the same kind as the Indian *potlatch*, that test the prestige and ability to dominate of the chiefs and elders. There are illustrations from Africa and Melanesia that show this very clearly. A new analysis of the cycles of *kula* exchange studied by Malinowski in the Trobriand Islands (Melanesia) shows that exchange regulated by precisely determined goods, reserved for this use alone, is primarily 'a mode of political organization'. The author of this revaluation, J. P. Singh Uberoi (*Politics of the Kula Ring*, 1962), reports that individual interests are expressed in *kula* goods and that subclans regarded as superior are situated in the richest village and play the most active part in the cycle. This example enables us to measure to what extent the political phenomenon may be masked; it hints that the long-standing search for the essence of the political is still far from concluded.

3. Political Power and Necessity

The notions of *power*, *coercion* and *legitimacy* are all interconnected and all necessary to this search. Why and how are they of fundamental importance? According to Hume, power is only a subjective category; not a datum, but a hypothesis that must be verified. It is not a quality inherent in individuals, but appears in an essentially teleological aspect – its ability to produce effects, by itself, on persons and things. Moreover, it is by its efficacy in this respect that it is defined. M. G. Smith believes that power is the ability to act effectively over people and things, using means ranging from persuasion to coercion. For Beattie, power is a particular category of social relations; it implies the possibility of constraining others within this or that system of relations between individuals and between groups. In this respect Beattie is following Weber, for whom power is the possibility given to an actor, within a determined social relation, of ruling as he wishes.

In fact, power – whatever forms condition its use – is recognized in every human society, however primitive. Because its existence is revealed above all in its effects, these should perhaps be examined before turning to its aspects and attributes. Power is always at the service of a social structure that can be maintained only by the intervention of 'custom' or law, by a sort of automatic conformity with the rules. Lucy Mair makes the useful remark that 'there is no society where rules are automatically obeyed' (1962, p. 18). Moreover, every society achieves only an approximate equilibrium; it is vulnerable. Anthropologists who have rid themselves of 'fixist' prejudices recognize this potential instability, even in an 'archaic' setting. The function of power, then, is to defend society against its own weaknesses, to keep it in good 'order', one might say; and, if necessary, to adapt itself to changes that are not in conflict with its basic principles. Lastly, as soon as the social relations extend beyond kinship relations, a more or less apparent *competition* is set up between individuals and groups, each trying to influence the decisions of the collectivity in accordance with his or its own particular interests. Consequently, political power appears as a product of competition and as a means of containing it.

A conclusion may be drawn from these initial remarks. Political power is inherent in *every* society: it arouses respect for the rules on which it is based; it defends the society against its own imperfections; it limits, within itself, the effects of competition between individuals and groups. It is these conservatory functions that get most consideration. Making use of a synthetic formula, *power may be defined, for every society, as resulting from the need to struggle against the entropy that threatens it with disorder* – as it threatens any system. But it must not be concluded that this defence has at its disposal only a single means – coercion – and can be ensured only by a clearly differentiated government. All the mechanisms that help to maintain or recreate internal cooperation must be considered. Rituals, ceremonies or procedures that ensure a periodical or occasional renewal of society, are instruments of political action in this sense just as much as rulers and their 'bureaucracy'.

Although power obeys *internal* determinisms that reveal it as a necessity to which every society is subjected, it seems none the less to result from an *external* necessity. Each total society is in relation with the world outside itself; it is, directly or at a distance, in relation with other societies that it regards as foreign or hostile, as a danger to its security and sovereignty. As a result of this external threat it is led not only to organize its defence and its alliances, but also to exalt its unity, cohesion and distinctive features. Power, which is necessary for the reasons of internal order considered above, takes form and is reinforced under the pressure of external dangers – real and/or supposed. Thus power and the symbols that are associated with it give society the means of affirming its internal cohesion and of expressing its 'personality', the means of protecting itself against and relating to the outside world. In his study of political representations, F. X. Sutton emphasizes the importance of symbols that distinguish one society from another and between 'representative' groups and individuals.

Certain circumstances provide a good illustration of this double system of relations, this double aspect of power, which is always directed both inwards and outwards. In a number of societies of the clan type, in which power remains a sort of diffused energy, the order of the political facts must be grasped as much by the examination of external relations as by the study of internal relations. An illustration of this may be found

among the Nuer of eastern Sudan. The different levels of expression of the political fact are defined in their society
primarily according to the nature of its external relations: a controlled opposition and arbitration between lineages linked by
the genealogical system, kinship or marriage; opposition and
controlled hostility (concerning only cattle) within the framework of relations between tribes; permanent mistrust of the
non-Nuer and war with a view to obtaining prisoners, cattle and
grain. In societies of another type, the double orientation of
power may be expressed in a *double polarization*. This is borne
out by a concrete example – from Africa, but there are others
elsewhere – that of the traditional chiefdom in the Bamiléké
country of the western Cameroons. The two dominant figures
of this society are the chief (*fo*) and the first dignitary (*kwipu*)
who plays the role of a warlord. The first appears as a factor of
unity, the guardian of the established order, the conciliator and
intercessor in relations with the ancestors and more active
deities. The second is concerned more with the external world,
with threats from outside and with ensuring the upkeep of the
military. These two powers are, in a sense, in competition, each
balancing the other; they form the two centres of the political
system. It can be seen, then, to what an extent internal and external factors are closely linked in the definition and organization of power.

This analysis would remain incomplete if a third condition
was not taken into account: power – however diffuse it may be
– implies a *dissymmetry* in social relations. If these relations were
established on the basis of perfect reciprocity, social equilibrium
would be automatic and power doomed to perish. But of course
this is not so; a perfectly homogeneous society, in which reciprocal relations between individuals and groups eliminated all
opposition and all division, appears to be an impossible society.
Power is strengthened by the accentuation of inequalities,
which are its precondition, just as it is the precondition of their
maintenance. Thus, the example of 'primitive' societies that
might be called egalitarian shows both the generality of the

fact and its most attenuated form. Positions of superiority and inferiority are established according to sex, age, genealogical situation, specialization and personal qualities. But it is in societies in which inequalities and hierarchies are apparent – suggesting rudimentary classes (proto-classes) or castes – that the relation between power and dissymmetries in social relations can be grasped in all clarity.

Political power has just been examined as a necessity and in reference to the internal order that it maintains and to the external relations that it controls. It has also been considered in its relation to one of the characteristics of all social structures: their more or less accentuated dissymmetry, their variable potentiality for inequality. We must now examine its two main aspects, its sacrality and its ambiguity.

In every society, the political power is never completely desacralized; and in the case of 'traditional' societies, the *relation with the sacred* is quite overt. But whether it is unobtrusive or apparent, the sacred is always present in political power. By means of this power society is seen as a unit (the political organization introduces the real totalizing principle), order and permanence. It is seen in an idealized form, as a guarantee of collective security and as a pure reflection of custom or law; it is experienced as a supreme, constraining value; it thus becomes the materialization of a transcendence imposed on individuals and particular groups. At this point, we might return to the argument used by Durkheim in his study of the elementary forms of the religious life. In his view, the relation of power with society is not *essentially* different from that between the Australian 'totem' and the clan. And this relation is obviously highly charged with sacrality. Anthropology is still largely, and often unconsciously, a sort of illustration of this fact.*

The *ambiguity* of power is no less evident. It appears as a necessity inherent in all social life and expresses the constraint exerted by the social life on the individual; it is all the more constraining in that it conceals an element of the sacred. It possesses

*Cf. Chapter 5, 'Religion and Power'.

therefore a great coercive capacity – so great, in fact, that it is regarded as *dangerous* by those subjected to it. As a result, certain societies possess a power from which its threats and dangers are eliminated. When P. Clastres expounds the philosophy of Indian chieftainship, he shows how this is achieved by an analysis of the political organization of most of the Amerindian societies. The theory implicit in these societies may be summarized in three propositions: power is essentially coercion; its transcendence presents a mortal danger to the group; the chief is obliged, therefore, at all times, to display the innocence of his function.

Power is necessary, but is confined within precise limits. It requires *consent* and a certain reciprocity. According to the regime this involves a network of highly varied responsibilities and obligations: peace and arbitration, the defence of custom and law, generosity, the prosperity of the country and of individuals, the agreement of the ancestors and gods, etc. In a more general way, it might be said that power must justify itself by maintaining a state of collective security and prosperity. This is the price to be paid by those who hold it – a price that is never wholly paid.

Consent implies both a principle (legitimacy) and mechanisms (those that contain abuses of power). Max Weber regards legitimacy as one of the fundamental categories of political sociology. He observes that no domination is content with mere obedience, but seeks to transform discipline into adhesion to the truth it represents – or claims to represent. He establishes a typology distinguishing the (ideal) types of legitimate domination: legal domination, which is rational in character; traditional domination, which is based on belief in the sacred character of traditions and in the legitimacy of power held in conformity with custom; charismatic domination, which is emotional in character and dependent on total confidence in an exceptional man, by virtue of his sanctity, his heroism or his exemplary character. All Weber's political sociology proceeds from these three modes of legitimizing the relation of command and obedience (cf.

Weber, 1969). It has inspired the theoretical approach of several anthropologists. Beattie distinguishes between power – in the absolute sense of the term – and political authority. Although the latter certainly implies 'public recognition' and 'acceptance', both presuppose legitimacy, which must be regarded as the distinctive criterion of authority. Hence a definition that emphasizes both these aspects: 'Social authority may be defined as the right, vested in a certain person or persons by the consensus of a society to make decisions, issue orders and apply sanctions in matters affecting other members of the society' (Beattie, 1959a, p. 99).

In one of his studies of the Tikopia of Polynesia, Raymond Firth examines in great detail the problem of 'acquiescence' and the effects of 'public opinion' (*Essays on Social Organization and Values*, 1964). He reminds us that power cannot be entirely autocratic. It seeks and receives a variable degree of support from the governed, either by routine apathy, inability to conceive of an alternative or acceptance of certain values regarded as unconditional. But in any case the governed impose limits on power; they try to contain it within certain bounds, by means of 'formal institutions' (chiefs' councils or nominated elders) or by 'informal mechanisms' (gossip and public opinion). We are back, then, at the ambiguity already mentioned: power tends to develop as a relation of domination, but the consent that legitimizes it tends to reduce its control. These contradictory movements explain that 'there can be no equilibrium in any political system'. Firth states emphatically: 'There is struggle, there are alliances; there is respect for the existing system and desire to change it; there is obedience to the moral law and attempt to get round it or reinterpret it to sectional advantage' (1964, pp. 143–4). Contrary to the Hegelian interpretation, the political does not necessarily realize the transcendence of particularities and particular interests.

Ambiguity, then, is a fundamental attribute of power. In so far as it depends on a more or less accentuated social inequality and guarantees the privileges of those who hold it, it is always, though to varying degrees, subject to contestation. At the same time it is accepted (as a guarantee of order and security), revered (by virtue of its sacred implications) and contested (because it justifies and maintains inequality). All political regimes express this ambiguity, whether they conform to tradition or to bureaucratic rationality. In African societies without a centralization of power – for example, those of the Fang and neighbouring peoples in Gabon and the Congo – corrective mechanisms that operate in secrecy threaten with death whoever abuses his authority or wealth. In certain traditional states of Black Africa, the tensions resulting from inequality are released in certain special circumstances – at such times, it seems, the social relations are suddenly and provisionally reversed. But the reversal is a controlled one: it is still organized within the bounds of the appropriate rituals, which may, in this respect, be *rituals of rebellion* in Max Gluckman's phrase. The supreme ruse of power is to allow itself to be contested *ritually* in order to consolidate itself more effectively.

4. Political Relations and Forms

In their book *Tribes without Rulers*, J. Middleton and D. Tait (1958) set out to define 'political relations' independently of the forms of government that organize them. They qualify these relations by the functions they perform: they are relations 'by which persons and groups exercise power or authority for the maintenance of social order within a territory' (1958, p. 1). They distinguish them according to orientation, internal or external; the first operate within the political unit, ensuring its cohesion, maintenance or adaptation; the second operate between distinct political units and are essentially of an antagonistic kind. There is nothing new here, of course. Radcliffe-Brown had already identified political relations by the regulation of force that they set up, and showed that they may operate both in relations between groups and within groups.

On the basis of his own experience in research – among the centralized societies of East Africa – and using an analytical method, J. Maquet distinguishes three orders of relations, which may be found together in the political process and which have a common formal characteristic, the importance of which has already been explained: they are clearly dissymmetrical. Maquet constructs three relational models composed of three elements – the actors, the roles and the specific content. He presents them in the following form:

	Elementary model of the political relation	Elementary model of social stratification	Elementary model of the feudal relation
Actors	Governors and governed	Superior, equal and inferior according to position in the order of strata	Lord and dependent
Role	To command and obey	To know how to behave according to one's status	Protection and services
Specific content	Physical coercion legitimately used	Rank	Interpersonal agreement

Maquet goes on to say that these models have a practical value; above all, they help in the classification of data and in the development of a comparative study, which is only realizable at a certain level of abstraction. He points out, quite rightly, that functions and relations are not linked in a simple, straightforward way: one cannot use the first to differentiate and compare the second in a rigorous fashion. He shows that the traditional states examined – those of the interlacustrian region of East Africa – are differentiated by the treatment imposed on each of his models and by the variable combinations that they produce from the three fundamental relations.* But the problems can only be grasped in a formal way.

The difficulties inherent in the analytical approach have already been examined; this approach separates elements that have meaning only by virtue of their situation in a real or logically constituted whole. Attempts to isolate and define an order of 'political' relations are soon confronted by their own limitations. It is true that Weber sets out with a fundamental relation, that of command and obedience, but he constructs his political sociology by seeking all the possible different ways in which that relation can be conceived and formulated. In order not to impoverish the content of the relation he places it in a wider context – that of the various forms of organization and justification of 'legitimate domination'. Modern anthropologists have come up against the same obstacles. They have studied political systems and organizations, aspects, modes of action and processes regarded as political; they have not been able, in a rigorous and useful way, to determine political relations. M. G. Smith remarks that this notion is of a substantive, rather than a formal character. The 'substance' that differentiates them from other categories of social relations can only be discovered by an elucidation of the nature of the political phenomenon. For this very reason, political philosophy cannot be dismissed by political anthropology as easily as Evans-Pritchard and Fortes imply in their introduction to *African Political Systems*.

Moving from the analytical to the synthetic level – that of the forms of political organization – the questions of method and terminology are no less difficult, even if one considers that the distinction between 'tribal' and 'political' societies is outmoded. In fact, there is a predominance of wide interpretations,

*Unpublished reports of the Groupe de Recherches en Anthropologie et Sociologie Politiques (1965).

and Schapera provides an accepted definition when he states that 'government in its formal aspects always involves the direction and control of public affairs by one or more specific persons whose regular function this is' (1956, p. 39). *All* societies, therefore, are concerned, but there is need for a distinction between different forms of government. The search for criteria of classification brings us up against the same difficulties met with in determining the political field.

The degree of differentiation and concentration of power is a criterion still frequently used. In particular, it is to be found in Lucy Mair's distinction between three types of government. At the lower level is *minimal government* – 'minimal' in three senses: the narrowness of the political community, the small number of those who hold power and authority, the weakness of power and authority. Next comes *diffused government*. This is based, in principle, on the entire adult male population, but certain institutions (such as age groups) and the holders of certain posts (possessing circumstantial authority) are responsible, in law and in fact, for the running of public affairs. The most elaborate form, based on a clearly differentiated and more centralized power, is that of *State government*. This triple typology transcends the contested (and now rejected) division of societies into those 'with a state' and those 'without a state'; but by establishing only broad categories, it requires the determination of sub-types that may multiply to excess and prove lacking in scientific usefulness. It lends itself no more easily than previous typologies to a simple classification of concrete political societies; because these societies – as Leach has shown in his study of the Kachin – may oscillate between two polar types and possess a hybrid form; because the same ethnic unit – that of the Ibo of southern Nigeria, for example – may use varied modalities of political organization. Moreover, every typology, because it sets up discontinuous types, is ill-equipped to deal with transitions. Lucy Mair implicitly recognizes this by considering 'the expansion of government' before studying the well constituted traditional states. In an article devoted to political organization among the American aborigines, Lowie had already shown that 'a genetic view of political structure must reckon with the fact that primeval anarchy could not suddenly blossom forth into a modern state' (1948b, p. 11B).

Easton, reviewing the difficulties met with in any typological search, suggests establishing 'a continuum of types' possessing a descriptive character rather than a deductive content. He attempts to do this by using the criterion of the differentiation of political roles: differentiation in relation to other social roles, between these roles themselves and by reference to the specific or diffused functions they perform. He tries to construct a 'three-dimensional scale of differentiation'. But the progress achieved by re-establishing continuity may be lost at the level of meanings. Easton recognizes this when he remarks: 'If a classification of systems along these lines is to have any utility . . . it must improve our understanding of how different types of systems operate' (1959, p. 243). This is tantamount to affirming that no typology has meaning in itself.

Max Weber has established ideal types that have served as definitions for certain specialists confronting the field of political anthropology. The criterion of classification has already been examined: it is the form taken by 'legitimate domination', which does not necessarily depend on the existence of the state. The type of *legal domination* is best illustrated by *bureaucracy*; and anthropologists like Lloyd Fallers (in *Bantu Bureaucracy*, 1956) have interpreted the modern developments of traditional political structures as ensuring the transition of a 'patrimonial' system of authority to a bureaucratic system. The type of *traditional domination*, in which personal relations are used exclusively as a support for the political authority, takes various forms: *gerontocracy* (which links power with seniority), *patriarchalism* (which maintains power within a particular family), *patrimonialism* and *sultanism*. The most widespread aspect is that known as patrimonial. Its norm is custom, regarded as inviolable, its mode of authority is essentially personal and its organization entails no administration in the modern sense. It employs dignitaries rather than functionaries; there is no separation between the private and the public sphere. It is the form of traditional domination most frequently encountered in the works of anthropologists. *Charismatic domination* is an exceptional type. It is a revolutionary form of power, a means of overthrow that operates against regimes of a traditional or legal character. Messianic movements with political implications, which have proliferated in recent years in Black Africa and Melanesia, illustrate this corrosive power that attacks the traditional order and introduces utopian fervour.

This 'ideal', non-descriptive typology seems equally vulnerable. In varying combinations it must combine different criteria; the nature of power, the mode of holding power, the gap between private and official relations, the degree of potential dynamism, etc. It cannot characterize the political types univocally. Moreover, it sets up oppositions – between the rational and the traditional, between these categories and that of the charismatic – which contradict the factual data and alter the nature of politics. The three elements are always present, if unequally accentuated – a generalization that is verified in the results obtained in the field of political anthropology.

Although political anthropology provides the means of undertaking a wider comparative study, it has not solved the problem of the classification of political forms in all their historical and geographical diversity. This inadequacy is apparent as soon as one examines societies with centralized power. The frontier between political systems based on chieftainship and monarchical systems is still not very rigorous. The size of the political unit is not enough to determine its broad outlines, though it has a direct effect on the organization of government: there are very large chiefdoms (those of the Bamiléké, in the Cameroons, for example). The coincidence of political space and cultural space – that is, the existence of a double unitary structure – does not constitute a distinctive criterion either; it is as exceptional in chiefdom societies as in traditional kingdoms. The same uncertainty is to be found when one examines the complexity of the politico-administrative apparatus: that of the Bamiléké chiefdoms is less complex than that of the sovereigns of Central and East Africa. The elements of differentiation are of another kind. The chief and the king differ not only in the extent and intensity of the power they exercise, but also in the nature of that power. Lowie suggests as much in his analysis of the political organization of the Amerindians. He contrasts the 'titular chief' with the 'strong chief', as illustrated by the Inca emperor. The first does not fully control the use of force (his function is often distinct from that of the war chief), does not legislate (but sees to the maintenance of custom) and has no monopoly of executive power. He is characterized by his gifts of oratory (the power of persuasion), his ability as a peacemaker and generosity. The 'strong chief', on the other hand, possesses coercive power and complete sovereignty; he is a sovereign in the full sense of the term. On the other hand, the criterion of social stratification is relevant to the distinction between chiefdom societies and monarchical societies. In the latter, the system of orders, castes (or pseudo-castes) and classes (or proto-classes) forms the main framework of society and inequality governs all predominant social relations within it. As a result, political typology must use means of differentiation that do not belong only to the political order.

Similar difficulties occur when one tries to classify clearly constituted states. The existence of one or several centres of power defines the two commonly used categories: 'centralized monarchies' and 'federative monarchies' (Eisenstadt, 1959). This rough division is of only limited utility, if only by virtue of the rarity of the second type – the political organization of the Ashanti of Ghana is often cited as an example. In a comparative study of African kingdoms, Vansina proposes a typology that is presented as 'a classification of structural models'. This essay clearly reveals the unresolved problems of method inherent in such an attempt. He uses five types which, in fact, are characterized by *heterogeneous* criteria: despotism, the clan kinship of the sovereigns and subordinate chiefs, the incorporation and subordination of 'ancient' powers, an aristocracy possessing a monopoly of power and, lastly, a federative organization (1962). Vansina is unable to confine himself to the two 'inter-linked' criteria that he at first chose: the degree of centralization and the rule of accession to power and political authority. It could hardly be otherwise in view of the diversity of forms taken by the traditional state *and* the multiple aspects – of unequal scientific interest – by which their classification may be made. According to the interpretation given to the political phenomenon, one or other of them must prevail; the degree of concentration and the mode of organization of power, the nature of the social stratification that determines the division into governors and governed, the type of relation to the sacred on which the legitimacy of all 'primitive' government is based. These three orders of typology are possible, but they do not have the same practical value.

It is obvious that the diversity of political organizations is more recognized than known and mastered scientifically. What are the reasons for this failure? The fact that work in the field of political anthropology is of recent origin – both in terms of descriptive field research and theoretical development – is the most obvious one. But it is not the most serious one. If one undertakes to define and classify types of political systems, one constructs models which serve to show in what way societies are similar or different in their power structure and which make it possible to study the transformations that explain the change from one type to another. The failures that occur in this field give rise to a fundamental question: do anthropology and sociology possess models that are adequately adapted to political forms?

The answer for the moment is no. While ever a knowledge of political relations and processes has not progressed by a systematic examination of their many manifestations, the difficulties will remain as insurmountable as ever. The very nature of political phenomena will constitute for a long time the main obstacle, if one admits that these phenomena are characterized by their *synthetic* aspect (they are identical with the organization of society as a whole) and by their *dynamism* (they are based on inequality and competition). The models necessary to their classification must, if they are to be adequate, be capable of expressing relations between heterogeneous elements and of taking into account the internal dynamisms of systems. It is because of this double necessity that the classificatory models developed by the structuralist anthropologists are unsuited to the study of the political sphere: they fulfil neither of these two conditions. The political can be reduced neither to a 'code' (such as language or myth) nor to a 'network' (such as kinship or exchange); it remains a total system that has not yet been given a satisfactory formal treatment. A realization of this fact is necessary to contain the ambitions of political anthropology in the fields of typology. For the moment, we should confine ourselves to the comparative study of related systems that represent, in a way, variations on the same 'theme' and belong to the same cultural region. This would make it possible to approach the problems of formalization – by testing a micro-typology – and to deepen our knowledge of the political, on the basis of a family of political forms linked to each other by culture and history.

Chapter Three

Kinship and Power

For many specialists, the order of kinship does not theoretically exclude the political order. According to Morgan's early definition, quoted in the previous chapter, the first regulates the state of *societas*, the second that of *civitas*, or, to use the currently fashionable anthropological terminology, the first refers to the structures of reciprocity, the second to the structures of subordination. In both cases, there is an obvious dichotomy. This dichotomy also appears in Marxist theory, in which class-society and the state are a result of 'the dissolution of the primitive communities' and in which the political emerges with the disappearance of 'personal blood-ties'. It is to be found, sometimes in original forms, in the tradition of philosophy, notably in the phenomenology of Hegel, who makes a parallel opposition between the universal and the particular, the state and the family, the masculine sphere (which is also the political and, therefore, superior sphere) and the feminine sphere.

Far from conceiving of kinship and the political as mutually exclusive terms, political anthropology has revealed the complex ties that exist between the two systems and has analysed and developed the theory of their relations on the basis of fieldwork. 'Lineage' or segmentary, acephalous or non-state societies, in which there is little differentiation between political functions and institutions, provided the first testing ground. In fact, it was in relation to these societies that the frontier between kinship and politics was opened up. Thus the study of lineage organization and its projection in space reveals quite clearly the existence of political relations based on the descent principle, outside the narrow framework of kinship. Similarly, kinship provides the principle with a model and a language in these societies, as Van

Velsen shows in the case of the Tonga of Malawi: 'political relations are *expressed* in terms of kinship' and the 'manipulations' of kinship are one of the means employed in political strategy. Lastly, in state societies, the two orders of relations often seem complementary and antagonistic, and the modalities of their co-existence had already been considered by Durkheim in a commentary devoted to a monograph on Ganda society published in 1911.* None of these manifestations must be neglected in an analysis of the relation between kinship and power.

1. Kinship and Lineages

Fortes has observed that the study of the relations and groups traditionally regarded from the point of view of kinship become more fruitful if examined from that of political organization. This is not to suggest, however, that kinship as a whole possesses political meanings and functions, but rather that the internal mechanisms of kinship, such as the formation of groups based on unilineal descent, and the external relations, such as the formation of networks of alliances based on matrimonial exchanges, set up and involve political relations. However, it is not easy to distinguish these relations, on account of the close ties between kinship and the political in many 'primitive' societies. One of the initial tasks, then, is to find criteria that will make such a distinction possible. The principle that determines adherence to a political community is one of these criteria. Just as the mode of descent – patrilinear or matrilinear – mainly conditions 'citizenship' in these societies, the relations and groups that it sets up are, in contrast with kinship in the strict sense of the term, political. In segmentary societies possessing a system of domestic slavery, the status of the slave defined first in terms of exclusion – from a lineage and from any share in the control of

---

*The monograph by J. Roscoe, *The Baganda*; it concerns a state society in Uganda. Durkheim's commentary appeared in *L'Année Sociologique*, vol. 12, 1912.

public affairs – reveals clearly this function of the mode of descent.

Lineages are based on men who, situated in the same genealogical framework, are linked unilineally to the same stock. Their extent varies according to the number of generations involved (the genealogical depth), as does the number of elements (or 'segments') that compose them. From the structural point of view, then, lineage groups are 'segmentary'. From a functionalist point of view, however, they are 'corporate groups', to use the term invented by British anthropologists; they hold symbols common to all their members, prescribe distinctive practices and oppose each other, in a sense, as differentiated units. Their political significance is primarily a consequence of this characteristic for their political role is determined more on the basis of their mutual relations than on the internal relations that constitute them. The ways in which the different elements are reconciled, the types of confrontation and conflict and the systems of alliance and territorial organization are in correlation with the general arrangement of the lineage segments and lineages.

An example from early anthropology will illustrate and develop these facts. The Tiv of Nigeria created a segmentary society incorporating a high number of individuals (over 800,000). A common genealogy going back to the founding ancestor – Tiv – embraces them all, in principle, according to patrilinear descent. It governs a 'pyramidal' structure containing lineages of variable extension: the genealogical level at which the referential ancestor is situated determines the size of the lineage group, which is called *nongo*. This structure does not operate mechanically, but according to a formula of alternate oppositions and solidarities; the homologous groups springing from the same stock are in opposition among themselves ($-$), but are associated together ($+$) within the immediately superior unit, which itself is in a relation of opposition with its homologues; the following diagram suggests this dynamic revealed by real confrontations.

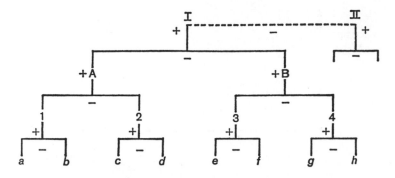

Articulation by alternate oppositions and solidarities

The political implication of these relations has been noted in all the societies conforming with this model, as has the role of conflict and war as *revealing* the units engaged in political life.

In Tiv territory these units are also expressed in a more permanent way in a highly demarcated spatial framework. Lineage groups of a certain size are associated with a definite territory, the *tar*; thus the segmentary structure of society involves a segmentary structure of space and, by successive articulations, the first incorporates the entire population and the second coincides with the entire territory. To the *tar*, a geographical unit, corresponds a political unit, the *ipaven*. Thus a close connexion is established between the descent groups called (*ityŏ*), lineage groups, territorial divisions and the political entities. A simplified diagram (see overleaf) might make these connexions clearer.

The descent principle and the territorial principle both contribute, in this case, to the determination of the political field, but the first is predominant. L. Bohannan emphasizes this fact when she says the descent group to which a Tiv belongs fixes his 'political citizenship, his rights to land and residence' (1958, p. 38), while at the same time defining the persons to whom he

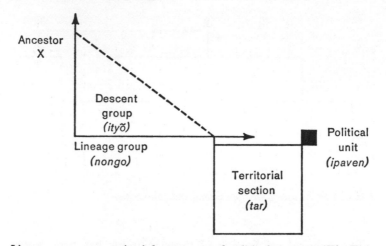

Lineage structure, territorial structure and political structure (The Tiv)

may be united by marriage.* The multiple functions of the descent groups and lineage groups always make it difficult to define the *strict* limits between the sphere of kinship and the political sphere. The Tiv establish the distinction by means of the territorial criterion. The simple residential units, which also differentiate the groups of production, organize the division of individuals according to kinship, but the territorial divisions, because they possess the *tar* quality, also have an essentially political character.

This simplified analysis, which would be echoed in studies of other segmentary societies, helps us to understand the uncertainty of the anthropologists – and the permanence of their disagreements. Although it is true, as Gluckman remarks, that there is room for a more detailed knowledge of political forms, the definition of the political, the apprehension of its specific aspects is still to be determined in societies with little differentiation, based on kinship and lineage order. This brings us back, in different terms, to the question already examined in the comparison between maximalists and minimalists.

*L. and P. Bohannan have published some remarkable studies of Tiv society (cf. particularly 1953).

In this respect, M. G. Smith has carried out the most systematic theoretical work. He sets out with one observation – the difficulty of determining the political (in segmentary societies) in terms of social groups and often imprecise frontiers – and one aim – the elimination of terminological confusions and the development of a more rigorous methodology. His theory was examined in the previous chapter; we must now consider its application to lineage and segmentary systems. According to this theory, the *external* relations of a lineage are primarily political relations, whether directly (in the case of war or feud) or indirectly (by matrimonial exchanges, rituals, etc.). *Internal* relations are primarily administrative relations; they are based on authority, on a hierarchy that gives a precise arrangement to social relations. Smith affirms – without, according to some critics, demonstrating it – that the internal mechanisms that help to reduce 'the latent dangers of conflict' may be regarded as rudimentary administrative mechanisms. The two dimensions of the political field are thus revealed; and the segmentary lineage system appears as 'a particular combination of administrative and political actions within and between structures defined formally in terms of unilineal descent' (1956, p. 53). But it is important to add that these two aspects (segmentation/hierarchy, power/authority) overlap in the lineage system; they are differentiated by reference not so much to the social groups as to the various 'levels' of the system and to the situations involving one or other of its elements.

In societies of this type the charter determining political positions is essentially the genealogical structure – which may be manipulated to legitimize a *de facto* power. And the political life is primarily revealed by the alliances and confrontations, the fusions and fissions that affect the lineage groups through rearrangements to the territorial structures. In his article 'Political anthropology', Easton insists on different and complementary characteristics. He emphasizes the instability of the 'support structures', which are formed by 'varying kinds of alliances and combinations among the segments'. These segments 'undergo relatively frequent subdivision, and typically readjust their alliances with equal ease' and there is 'a constant challenge to the political leadership' (1959, pp. 231-2). Political struggle acquires from this fact a special character; it is aimed not at changes to the system, but at a new adjustment of its constitutive elements; it is expressed in terms of secessions, regroupings or new conditions. Easton remarks that this mechanism of segmentary societies might justify viewing 'each lineage . . . as an independent political system. Competition for power on the part of the lineage . . . as equivalent to behaviour in foreign relations' (1959, p. 235-6). The character of the political system would then be seen in its most simplified and most unstable form.

In an article containing a critical inventory, H. M. Fried re-examines the remaining imprecisions and ambiguities (1957). Descent groups – entities that make it possible to situate individuals and reconstruct lines of descent from a single ancestor – must be distinguished from real lineage groups, which appear as 'corporate groups' in certain circumstances and are often localized; and, in turn, these lineage groups must be distinguished from clans, which are usually defined in relation to a distant (and often mythical) ancestor and whose internal articulations cannot all be rediscovered. Moreover, when the lineages are subjected to a precise localization, they do not, by this fact, constitute communities; they are only the 'kernel' of such communities – women being exported by the play of marriage and wives being received from outside; they remain closely linked to kinship relations and are thus, in Leach's term, 'compromise groups'. At this level, kinship, economics and politics are intermingled and politics appears only somewhat intermittently. The formal analysis of lineage structures is not enough to reveal their political characteristics; indeed, Fried is forced to increase the criteria of identification and to give an important role to the criteria of rank and stratification – that is, to inequalities of status and of access to strategic resources.

Moreover, too rigid a differentiation between kinship and the political sphere leads to a neglect of the political effects of the former, in particular its possible uses in the play of competition. The capitalization of wives, descendents and alliances is a frequent means of strengthening (or maintaining) power. There are more complex correlations. Godfrey Lienhardt, comparing the Nilotic societies (East Africa), which are all patrilinear, but with unequally differentiated political power, reveals the triple relation between the degree of centralization, the intensity of competition and the importance given to matrilateral kinship. The third of these serves as a support for enterprises concerned with the conquest of power; more often, this possibility becomes more valuable the more competition hardens and the resulting power increases. There are also symbolic correlations. A break in the bonds of kinship (incest or the murder of a parent) is often believed to have been at the origin of traditional kingships: in establishing his power and building up a new order the founder seems to exclude himself from the old order; historical myths and royal rituals recall this 'event' and thus express the exceptional nature of the sovereign.

2. The Lineal Dynamic

The difficulties met with in the determination of the political field, outside kinship, and in the application of the structural analysis of the political to segmentary societies are reason enough for a fresh attack on the problem. Present-day research takes less account of the formal aspects than of the situations and revealing dynamisms, the strategies and manipulations of power and authority. It pays more attention to the conditions necessary to the expression of the political life, its ways and means.

a. The conditions

The 'segmentary' are neither egalitarian nor devoid of relations of pre-eminence and subordination. The clans and lineages are not all equivalent; the clans may be differentiated, specialized and 'ordered'; the lineages may confer unequal rights according to whether they concern an elder or a junior; both may be distinguished for the requirements of ritual order, which involve political and economic effects.

Even the Nuer of the Sudan, who form a kind of extreme case by reducing unequal relations to a minimum, have not eliminated them altogether; though they exist in their society perhaps in a more latent than an effective way. In the various territorial sections, a leading clan or lineage occupies a predominant position; Evans-Pritchard calls such a clan or lineage 'aristocratic' (on account of its superior status), but he adds 'its predominance gives prestige rather than privilege' (Evans-Pritchard and Fortes, 1946, p. 287). During the initiation of adolescent boys, lineages possessing a ritual prerogative – those formed by the 'men of the cattle' – provided the dignitaries whose responsibility it is to open and close the cycle; they intervene therefore in a system that ensures the socialization of individuals and divides them into 'classes' with differentiated status – those of the seniors, the equal and the juniors; they play a political role. Lastly, a particular ritual function, that of 'leopard skin' elder, also belongs to certain lineages outside the dominant clans; it carries with it the position of conciliator in grave differences and of mediator in those concerning cattle. It too has political implications. Inequalities and specializations, whether clan or lineal, the three statuses resulting from the system of age groups, and differences or inequalities in access to land and cattle define Nuer political life quite as much as oppositions and coalitions between lineal and territorial units. Evans-Pritchard suggests as much and goes on to say that the most influential men are characterized by their clan position (they are aristocrats) and lineal position (they are heads of extended families), by their age group (they have the status of elders), by their wealth (in cattle) and their 'strong personality'. In the absence of a well differentiated political authority, pre-eminence, prestige and influence result from a combination of these minimal inequalities. In the absence of a distinct political power, a politico-religious power – predominantly religious – operates by the interplay of clan-lineage structures, territorial structures and age-groups. It cannot be defined by these structures alone, but rather by the unequal relations on which it is based and the dynamic of the oppositions and conflicts by which it is expressed.

A second example from Africa – that of the Tiv, a society of the same type as the previous one – enables us to carry the analysis further. Lineages and kinship, territorial divisions and age groups provide the main fields of social relations; but the examples of inequality and the centres of political life are more apparent. Outside the system are the slaves: they belong to no age group, are excluded from the sphere of public affairs and remain in a dependent situation. Within the system, there are distinctions between the pre-eminent men (whose names serve to identify the lineal and age groups), men who possess 'prestige' (by virtue of their material success and their generosity) and the political guides (called *tyo-or*) who complement the previous two. The first owe their influence to their lineal position, their position as elders and their magico-religious powers, which condition the maintenance of a state of health and fertility and the maintenance of order. The second are in a position of power for economic reasons. Indeed, the additional influence that results from the possession of a market place expresses this political aspect of situations acquired within the Tiv economy – the competition for the place of market master is one of the forms of political struggle. The 'political guides' are not holders of a permanent office, but are concerned with *external* relations: they make their appearance at times of arbitration or peace negotiations with other similar groups.

For the Tiv, who do not possess a special term for the

political sphere, political action takes place by means of kinship and lineages, age groups and the relations produced by the market system; it is not expressed in a particular language, but in the language proper to each of its means. One may rightly speak of diffused government and of a diffused political life, subjacent to all relations between individuals and groups, that is revealed not by specific institutions, nor even by any social forms through which it might operate, but by various dynamisms – of competition and domination, coalition and opposition. The political may be reduced to its minimal expression, but it retains none the less its characteristic as a dynamic system. Indeed, Tiv theory suggests as much. According to this theory, legitimate power depends on the possession of a mystical quality (called *swem*) that ensures peace and order, the fertility of agriculture and of women, and is expressed in the vigour of its possessor. This quality, which, in a way, is the substance of power and the force of order, nevertheless involves struggles for its seizure and its misuse. On the other hand, rivalries for prestige and influence, and attempts to broaden the political role or increase one's material well-being are always interpreted in the language of sorcery. The dangerous substance known as *tsav*, which such actions set free, reveals power from the point of view of the struggles and inequalities on which it is based. The Tiv believe that men accede to power 'by devouring the substance of others'.* This indigenous theory ignores neither the dynamic nor the ambiguity of the political – which is, at the same time, in precarious equilibrium, the creator of order and the bearer of disorder.

Outside Africa, segmentary societies reveal similar conditions of intervention on the part of the political life. This is the case of the Melano-Polynesian area, where the strongly constituted state is an exceptional form of the organization of government. The Tikopia of Polynesia, studied by Firth, are divided into about twenty patrilineages, which are linked to each other by various procedures to form four clans. At the head of each clan

*A belief mentioned by P. Bohannan.

is a 'chief', who is drawn from a single lineage that gives all its members a superior status; and the four chiefs, who are differentiated by specific ritual functions, are classed according to an order of pre-eminence that is not identified with a political hierarchy. The clans do not have equal relations between themselves, and still less do the lineages, which may be differentiated outside the genealogical framework by differences of rank. Below the small group of clan chiefs, Tikopia society reveals two series of pre-eminence on which the 'authority structure' is based. The first is that of the *pure* – the elders – who are at the head of the major lineages. Their position results from both their genealogical position *and* the good will of their clan chief. They are regarded as the 'symbolic fathers' of the lineages and their function is essentially of a ritual character. They are not equal, but are placed in a *ritual* hierarchy that reproduces that of the deities they serve; only the more elevated of them contribute to the maintenance of public order. The second series of pre-eminences is that of the *maru*. It is justified by rank and not by acquaintance with the gods – for it is a result of birth and requires that one should be the brother, close agnatic cousin or son of the chief – and confers unquestionable authority – the role of carrying out the chief's orders and of maintaining peace and security. Whereas the clan chief possesses a political power deriving from his religious position (control of the *kava* ritual associated with the lineage system, possession of 'physical purity' and 'moral purity'), the *maru* elder possesses only a delegated, laicized authority.

In this framework, the lineal dynamic results from the inequality in rank. Firth sees these inequalities as fundamental: 'With rank comes power and privilege, and with these the possibilities for oppression.' He suggests that the political is all the more apparent in Tikopia society in that a 'hierarchical class structure' is built up on the segmentary structure determined by kinship and descent. He reports that 'class' interests and conflicts latent within the 'classes' are recognized in indigenous theory. Thus the political system linking the chiefs, the *maru* notables and the 'elders', between each other and with the people, is revealed as a system of complementary – and in certain circumstances antagonistic – forces. Firth concludes his analysis by affirming that there can be no equilibrium in any political system, thus emphasizing the essentially dynamic character of the political (1964, chapters 5 and 6).

A last example, from Melanesia, will enable us to extend these variations on a theme. The New Caledonian societies of the 'Great Land' and the surrounding islands, while possessing the same basic patterns, present complex and diversified forms. The social basis is formed by relations of kinship and descent, by the networks resulting from matrimonial exchanges and by the 'systematic relationships' set up between the groups recognized as clans (Guiart, 1963). These clans play the principal role in political life: they operate in the field of coalitions and oppositions; they serve as a framework for the hierarchy of status and prestige on which power is based. Indeed, Guiart sees them as 'a complex phenomenon belonging both to the network and the hierarchy'. The clan (*moaro*) is determined according to several criteria. It is defined by genealogies (it refers to a male stock and to its agnatic descent by localization), a vital, sacred link connects it to a particular territory, by symbols (name, totem) and the possession of specific gods, and by the relations of filiation, adoption or dependence maintained with other groups. But reality is less precise than this definition would lead one to believe: local groups are unstable because of the successive outbursts that involve 'the geographical dispersal of lineages'; identification and allegiances are maintained in spite of distances; foreign elements are introduced into local structures.

The conditions of political power are to be found both in the dynamic proper to the clan and in the characteristic inequalities of a society of the 'aristocratic type' (Guiart) – though, even in its most elaborate political organizations, it does not go beyond the stage of 'great chiefdom'. Social status is determined by one's proximity to the revered ancestor and to the 'elder line', which maintains power in its own hands. 'At the lower limit,' says Guiart, 'the pariah might be a direct, but distant agnatic relation of the supreme chief.' The position of 'the father–eldest son pair of the eldest branch'* at the head of the chiefdom confirms this rule governing clan inequality and hierarchy. The relation to the land, one element in the definition of a clan, is also a factor of inequality: the possession of the earliest inhabited land confers 'the most authentic claims to nobility' (cf. Leenhardt, 1930); the inhabitants of longest standing have the best land, to the detriment of newcomers, and this 'contradiction' is 'an essential aspect of the dynamism of society'. In a general way, individual conditions are seen in terms of superiority and inferiority: chiefs/subjects, 'great men'/'little men', *orokau* (holders of power and prestige)/*kamoyari* (juniors and members of subordinate lineage groups).

New Caledonian society tends to set up an equilibrium between those of different status, but it does not succeed in eliminating the contradictions on which it is based and which, at the same time, threaten its existence. These contradictions are reflected in the person of the chief and in the organization of the chiefdom. At the head of the clan is the 'great son' (*orokau*), for whom all the members of the clan are 'brothers', in the classificatory sense of the term – though the ideology of brotherhood does not succeed in concealing the relation of domination that places the chief outside the bounds of kinship and establishes a power that the earliest observers regarded as despotic. The chiefdom is based on a duality of power: although the chief (*orokau*) imposes his will by speech, orders in both senses of the term and enjoys prestige, the master of the land (*kavu*), the holder of relations with the gods, possesses a less overt but effective authority and influences the decisions of the chief. This dualism suggested by the pairs of oppositions that it implies – political/religious, foreign/indigenous, dynamism/conservatism – reveals a contradiction that 'constitutes a good deal of the dynamism of the institution' (Guiart). These facts are the most obvious, but they should not exclude the many differentia-

*A phrase used by P. Métais (1956).

tions and oppositions established according to positions of genealogy, status, property and ritual. They are the constitutive elements of the political life; they are resolved into 'an equilibrium of factors making for coherence and reasons making for anarchy'.

Despite the simplification of the analysis, this last example confirms previous observations. It shows that the dynamic character of the political is as important as (more so in this case than) the formal aspect. Thus, by its ambiguity and the multiplicity of its manifestations, the political reveals its diffused presence in societies that have been unable to establish a unitary government. But a more essential lesson may be drawn from these comparisons. The societies considered here manage to function only by using the energy created by the differences in condition between individuals (according to their status) and the social distance established between groups (according to their situation within an often rudimentary hierarchy). They use the inequality of opportunity created by the genealogical, ritual and economic inequalities – the first two rather than the last because of the low level of technical and economic development. They transform disequilibrium and conflict – at their reduced scale – into an agent for social cohesion and order; to this end, the political is already and necessarily their instrument. However, the transformation of opposition into cooperation, disequilibrium into equilibrium, can always break down, and certain procedures or rituals ensure, in a way, a periodical recharging of the political machine. But indigenous theories (those of the Tiv, for example) do express a permanent fear that disorder will not be contained by order and that power will become a means for evil.

b. Revealers and means

In 'segmentary' societies, the diffused political life is revealed more by *situations* than by political institutions. These are, in fact, the societies in which the political structures are least 'visible' and most 'intermittent', to use Almond's terms. The making of decisions concerning the community creates pre-eminent men, men of superior rank, elders' councils, temporary or established chiefs. Individual conflicts that necessitate the intervention of law and custom and the redressing of wrongs, antagonisms that lead to a feud or to war are all circumstances that reveal the mediators and holders of power. The analysis of the Nuer and Tiv systems suggests this. I. M. Lewis's study of the Somali of East Africa (*A Pastoral Democracy*, 1961) shows, as an extreme example, the political function of oppositions intervening between groups constituted according to the descent principle. It is power relations – numerical superiority and military potential – that primarily govern relations between clans or between lineages and determine the extent of the various political units and their real hierarchy.

Covert confrontation is a revealer of the political life of lineage societies quite as much as direct confrontation. Some of these societies possess secret (but effective) mechanisms of limiting the holding of powers and the accumulation of wealth. Thus, the Gabonese Fang, among whom death threatens anyone who disrupts clan solidarity and the egalitarian tendency by satisfying his ambition and private interests, justify the means used to contain inequality. According to the traditional interpretation, the goods to which an individual may aspire (wives, descendants, produce, prestige symbols) exist only in a limited and constant number. Any abusive accumulation by one member of the clan or patrilineage must work to the detriment of all the others. Thus an exceptionally numerous progeny is believed to involve 'stealing' part of the progeny to which all the other men in the lineage group have a right. This egalitarian ideology underlies the procedures for the redistribution of material wealth, but its requirements are contradicted by reality. The *scarcity* of wealth and prestige symbols, on the one hand, and the difficulty of controlling individual attempts to seek wealth and power, on the other, create so obvious a contradiction that the privileged are placed in an ambiguous, or vulnerable position and the inegalitarian access to wealth is attributed to the use of witchcraft.

The dialectic of contestation and conformity, power claimed and power accepted, is generally expressed in the language of witchcraft, revealing indirectly a concealed opposition, when it is not merely a direct recourse to the practices of aggressive magic. Nadel opened the way to a similar interpretation when he presented the beliefs concerning witchcraft as symptoms of the tensions and anxieties that result from social life (in a comparative study of four African societies, published in 1952). The distinction offered by the British anthropologists between 'sorcery', or witchcraft by a technique available to anyone, and 'witchcraft' proper, which is dependent on an innate power and cannot be acquired, is a fundamental one. Witchcraft, in this sense, is present mainly in societies in which the descent principle governs basic relations; it predominates and is transmitted according to the mode of devolution of offices and functions. J. Middleton and E. H. Winter emphasize this fact in a collection of essays published under their editorship (*Witchcraft and Sorcery in East Africa*, 1963). They also reveal the ambiguity of these manifestations in relation to the 'chiefs' and the established order. They express the opposition of the non-privileged and the strategy of the ambitious, but they may also help to strengthen the political leadership by the fear that they inspire – a fear the leadership uses to its own advantage – and by the threat of an accusation that makes a witch-hunt one of the instruments of conformity and order. Thus, in the case of the Kaguru of Malawi, witchcraft not only expresses the antagonism between factions, but also helps to strengthen the position of the holders of power and privileges, some of whom are not afraid of enhancing their reputation as 'witch-doctors'.

Several societies of East Africa provide similar examples; the notables use witchcraft in order to ensure their pre-eminence and influence in the tribe or clan. Among the Nandi of Kenya, the dominant figure is the *orkoiyot*, who is neither a chief nor a judge, but a 'ritual expert' who intervenes decisively in tribal affairs. He is an ambivalent figure who combines beneficent qualities (including those of the divine) and the dangerous powers of the witch-doctor, which strengthen his ritual authority and the fear that he inspires. In so far as the *orkoiyot* is the equivalent of a chief, this double aspect of his person reflects the two faces of the political – that of a beneficent order and that of constraint or violence.

On the other hand, the opposite strategy may have similar results; witchcraft, identified unreservedly with disorder and absolute evil, is confused with every action that contradicts the norms and weakens the established order; it constantly threatens to turn against its user. For example, among the Gisu of Uganda, the risk of an accusation of witchcraft maintains respect for lineal pre-eminences and for the older generation, fear of non-conformity, and the generosity of those members of a lineage who have attained material success. Contestation and the rise of individuals with concurrent prestige is opposed, therefore, by the most effective of obstacles; witchcraft is not merely one of the instruments manipulated by the political leadership, but its most reliable protection, for it backfires on those who use it in opposition or rivalry.

The study of the lineal micro-societies of the Melanesian archipelagos shows with equal clarity the interlinking of relations of a political character and the complex relations that depend on witchcraft. The most illuminating demonstration of this is R. F. Fortune's classic work, *Sorcerers of Dobu* (1932). The Dobuans inhabit islands off the tip of New Guinea; there are not many of them (7000 at the time of the study) and they are divided into very small villages, which are linked with their neighbours to form endogamous units, which also act as alliances in war against similar units; they form matrilineages and each localized lineage group owns its own land. Their political system is so minimal that it has been regarded simply as the result of the permanent opposition between the various village coalitions. However, chieftainship does exist, at least in an 'embryonic' state, and an inequality of status differentiates the 'big men' from the others. Both witchcraft and sorcery have a part to play, as the title of Fortune's book suggests. The 'embryonic' chief is defined by his lineal position, his strong personality, his mastery of ritual and magic, and his great skill in the technique of sorcery; he is the most powerful man and strives to serve custom and the common good. The evil sorcerer appears as the internal enemy – he is dangerous simply on account of his geographical proximity; he symbolizes the rivalries and tensions operating within the groups of allied villages; he personifies the strict distinction between internal, covert conflicts (witchcraft) and external, overt conflicts (war), and the play of oppositions and alliances inherent in all political life.

Further illustrations would not alter the results of the preceding analyses. Witchcraft, like 'private war' (feud) and 'external war', is one of the principal revealers of the social and political dynamic of lineage societies. Each of these modalities of opposition and conflict operates in fields of relations which broaden as they pass from one to another, working outwards from the local community, that is, from the sphere governed above all by kinship to that controlled by the political. Witchcraft is also a means at the disposal of political power, whether it strengthens its constraint and/or protects it against contestation, or whether it allows a true transference, on to the accused or the suspect, of the resentments and doubts threatening the lineal authorities. Lastly, as Firth has pointed out, it is 'a way of saying something', a *language* expressing certain types of relations between individuals and social groups. In this sense, it constitutes the code used in political confrontations and provides the arguments that are employed by the political ideology implicit in clan societies.

Non-state societies have been called unanimist and regarded as basing every important decision on general consent. Above all, they have been seen from a mechanistic point of view that gives undue importance to the opposition and alliance of the segments of the various orders making up the political units.

The preceding observations show that reality is distorted by such simplified interpretations. The discovery of antagonisms, struggles and conflicts suggests the importance of political strategy in societies with minimal or diffused government and encourages one to point out the diversity of its means. The genealogical charter, kinship and marriage alliances may be transformed into instruments in the struggle for power, for they are never mere mechanisms that automatically ensure the attribution of political status and the devolution of office. The manipulation of the genealogies is more frequent than ethnographers – often victims of their devotion towards their informers – would suggest. A Cameroon writer, Mongo Beti, denounces the trickery used in the political struggle by ambitious rivals in his own society – that of the Beti, who belonged to the great Fang group. He sees the patri-clan (*mvõg*) as the unstable product of historical vicissitudes and genealogical references as the range of arguments justifying the clan dimension, which is better adapted to the circumstances. 'One will reveal oneself,' he says, 'unless one invents a common ancestry.' He emphasizes the dynamic character of the clan, the continual formation of patrilineages that aspire, under the leadership of enterprising men, first to independence, then to the status of clan unit. These men employ a well tried procedure that consists of creating an entourage of relations and dependents for oneself, then bringing about a secession that is finally recognized when the separated group is given a distinctive name – that of its founder.

In order to legitimize this new situation, genealogies are often rectified and clan identity is conferred on the members of the new group, who do not in fact possess it. The founder's political rise and the unity that he establishes is possible only on the basis of an initial capitalization of relations and 'clients', itself implying the possession of wealth and matrimonial powers used to the advantage of his dependents. What takes place, then, is a *total political enterprise* involving kinship, rights over women, wealth and genealogical conventions. The process that governs it may be summarized in the following table:

Phase 1 Capitalization of wealth and matrimonial powers

↓

Phase 2 Capitalization of relations and dependents

↓

Phase 3 Capitalization of prestige and influence

↓

Phase 4 Secession and genealogical legitimation

Lineage societies are the setting for a competition that frequently affects the established powers and often creates instability in the alliances between groups. Van Velsen shows this in his study significantly entitled *The Politics of Kinship*, in which he describes and analyses the society of the lakeside Tonga of Nyasaland. 'Effective political power and influence,' he says, 'do not necessarily or exclusively rest with those who are genealogically and thus constitutionally entitled to it' (1964, p. 78). The system of kinship and descent relations, he believes, forms a complex of relations that may be manipulated for private, economic and political ends, and the play of political ambition, by causing the formation of separate villages, constitutes a permanent threat for the 'chiefs', for they are chiefs by virtue not so much of their title as of the number of their 'followers'. Although in this precise group the spatial mobility of persons and groups expresses political instability, this instability is also to be found in the fluctuation of alliances formed between the clans and lineages.

The situation of the Siane of New Guinea, studied by R. F. Salisbury, is an excellent example in this respect. The patrilinear clans form villages and alliances that are so unstable that 'friends' may become 'enemies' within ten years. The competition that causes these changes in the positions of power and the hierarchies of prestige may lead to violence (war). But the aim of this violence is never conquest, but the seizure of rights by one clan from another, which is then placed in a position of inferiority. These confrontations are centred around the possession of women, wealth that is reserved for ceremonial exchanges and pigs, which have a ritual value. In this acephalous society the fluctuating political equilibriums result from a combination of war, alliances and the circulation of prestige symbols. They reveal not so much a quasi-automatic regulation as a strategy involving each clan and conforming to principles that define the hierarchies and powers of the Siane culture.

This example clearly shows the role played by the competitions over certain riches and certain symbols in the sphere of political rivalry. Lineage societies are those in which wealth is distinguished not so much by accumulation as by the generosity or challenges it arouses. Dorothy Emmet (1968) has shown the calculating, rather than disinterested, character of a generosity that in fact helps to determine the respective situations in the social scale and remains, in the last analysis, one of the obligations and means of power. E. Sapir has also remarked that superior positions may be conquered 'by means of potlatches and acts of prodigality', not only by 'individuals of base extraction', but also by lineage groups. The strategy of the use of wealth, which is directed towards economic ends, is aimed, *at the same time*, at all forms of social communication, including the hierarchies of prestige and power. It belongs to the sphere of political confrontations. The study of the Trobriand (Melanesia), continued by Singh Uberoi, confirms this thesis with remarkable rigour. The rank of a localized lineage depends on three factors: its economic ability, its quality as an 'integrating' centre for the economic activities of its neighbours and its position in the networks of alliances. This position is particularly revealed during the ritual exchanges of *kula*, which are objects reserved for this use alone. During the great *kula* expeditions (called *uvalaku*), the competition between lineages and villages is exacerbated. The political dynamic is freed to the degree that the lineage status depends on the capitalization of alliances and makes it possible to establish supremacy over the inhabitants of fertile regions. The order of the three factors determining the rank of lineages is inverted and the political link conditions economic advantage.

The strategy of the use of 'symbols' also acquires a political significance; this is shown by an examination of the relations between religion and power.* But a brief account of a particular case would deepen our understanding of this fact. In a work on the religious life of the Lugbara of Uganda, Middleton (1960) emphasizes the strength of the link between 'ritual and authority'. He remarks that the ritual behaviour of this people does not make sense if one forgets that the cult of the dead is intimately linked with the maintenance of lineage power, and that the conflicts surrounding this power are translated into mystical terms. He describes the rivalries between the elders, who are the holders of pre-eminences and are responsible for decisions, and the discontented 'juniors' as a confrontation centred on the ancestors' altars and ritual symbols. Moreover, this mode of political action is proper not only to lineage societies; it is also to be found in societies with strict stratification and differentiated government. Gluckman has shown this on the basis of several African monarchies and Leach on the basis of the Kachin, who choose, according to their particular situation, the most favourable mythical references for their present interest.

3. Aspects of 'Segmentary Power'

The 'segmentary' systems, which are now admitted to be political systems, have not yet been given an unquestionable classification based on political criteria. Their typology has remained difficult for two sets of reasons: their fundamental instability (power remains diffused or intermittent, political units changeable and alliances and affiliations precarious) and the variations that are sometimes found within the same ethnic group – for example in the case of the Ibo of southern Nigeria, where

*Cf. Chapter 5, 'Religion and Power'.

political power rests on different combinations of the lineage principle (patrilateral lineages), the age-group principle and the principle of association according to ritual specialization.

By overemphasizing the clan-lineage arrangements, and the genealogical structures that justify them, one may determine *types* based on the way in which this articulation is realized. Thus, in their Introduction to *Tribes without Rulers* (1958), Middleton and Tait make a correlation between the mode of organizing the genealogies that define the localized lineage groups, the degree of autonomy or interdependence of these groups, the degree of specialization of the political functions and the forms of violence used in case of conflict. They construct three classificatory models on the basis of comparatively studied African cases: (I) societies with a unitary genealogy and lineages integrated into 'a single pyramidal system'; (II) societies made up of small, interdependent descent groups; (III) societies made up of 'associated' lineages that cannot be placed within the same genealogical framework. A table of the main criteria (positive/+ or negative/—) makes it possible to place each of these types in relation with the others:

Criteria	Types		
	I	II	III
Genealogical depth	+	—	+
Unitary genealogy	+	—	—
Relative stability of the system	—	+	+
Interdependence of political units	—	+	—
Possible heterogeneity	—	—	+
Apparent chieftainship	—	—	+

Classificatory models of lineage systems

This mode of classification reveals significant differences (for example, the relations between the stability of the system and the interdependence of the political units, between the heterogeneity of these units and the differentiation of the chieftainship), but it remains unsatisfactory. It does not adequately take into account the dynamic proper to each of the models – the forms taken by political action and by the confrontations in which it is expressed. It is based too exclusively on the criterion of unilineal descent and on the genealogical code that defines the various segments; it ignores the other important criteria that intervene concurrently and which contribute to the political organization of the lineage societies. Fried (1957) tries to overcome this difficulty by increasing the criteria by which the unilineal descent groups are differentiated: explicit or implicit genealogical reference, the 'corporate' or 'non-corporate' character of the unit, the presence or absence of a hierarchy of ranks and of a stratification. Examining the case of the 'corporate' groups, Fried builds up, by combination, eight types of class or lineages:

Ranks	Stratification	Demonstrated descent	Types	Examples
−	−	−	Egalitarian clan	Northern Tongus
+	−	−	Ranking clan	Tikopia
−	+	−	Stratified clan	
+	+	−	Ranking and stratified clan	
−	−	+	Egalitarian lineage	Nuer
+	−	+	Ranking lineage	Tikopia
−	+	+	Stratified lineage	
+	+	+	Ranking and stratified lineage	China (the Tsu)

Unilineal Corporate Descent Groups
(Basic types according to M. H. Fried)

This attempt is useful in that it reveals the effect of stratification (though it limits its existence to certain societies) and hierarchies of rank on the clan and lineage systems. It takes into account, therefore, one of the conditions *necessary* for the expression of the political life – a condition that analyses centred on descent and alliance often ignore or underestimate. But the typology is simplified and of only limited scientific use. Lewis, in his essay 'Problems in the comparative study of unilineal descent groups' (1965) remarks on this fact and emphasizes the *various* functional significances of the descent principle, which does not always apply to society as a whole (because of a kind of national genealogy) and does not necessarily ensure political or religious cohesion, but defines the juridical unit within which arbitration and conciliation take place. Lewis also insists on the 'multiple characteristics' of unilateral descent and on the differences of emphasis that diversify one society from another. He shows that it does not operate as a political principle unique to segmentary societies and examines it in relation to other structural principles: local contiguity, organization by age-groups and cooperation of the contractual kind. A unilateral treatment of the facts cannot be satisfactory, for the very reason that it contradicts this observation. The political field must be seen in all its extent and complexity, even at the price of the vulnerability of any typology of segmentary political systems.

In a study examining 'primitive political systems' by the comparative analysis method, Eisenstadt (1959) sets out to establish the most relevant criteria. He finds four main ones: the degree of differentiation of the political roles, the dominant character of political activity, the nature and extent of the political struggle, the form and intensity of tolerable changes. By adapting his method to the case of the 'segmentary tribes', Eisenstadt tries to shift the point at which the analysis is applied: from the political aspects of kinship, descent and alliance to political manifestations themselves. He distinguishes six types.

1. The 'band', the simplest type of social and political organization, which is illustrated by the Australian tribes, the Pygmies and certain Amerindian tribes, etc.

2. The 'segmentary tribe', in which the political roles and offices are linked to the lineage groups; the emphasis is more ritual than political; competition operates between the lineages and the clan or lineage authorities.

3. The 'non particularist segmentary tribe', which dissociates political life from the sphere of kinship and descent; the link with territory, membership of an age-group or a regiment and the relation to the principal rituals determine the attribution of political functions: competition for office and 'dispute' over public affairs become apparent.

4. The 'tribe with associations', in which political offices are distributed between certain 'kinship groups', which have a monopoly of them, and between the various associations that characterize this type; these two series of groups, and those organized on a territorial basis, perform complementary functions, though without entirely eliminating tensions; there is rivalry above all between the associations; the Indian societies of North America (Hopi, Zuni, Kiowa) belong to this category.

5. The 'tribe with ritual stratification' (the Anuak of the Sudan and Ethiopia), in which differentiation and hierarchical order are expressed above all by reference to the 'symbolico-ritual field'; a division between aristocrats and commoners does exist, however, the former competing for the political offices, which are defined less by power than by ritual superiority.

6. The 'tribe with autonomous villages', which is based on the village or area; the political implications of kinship and descent are reduced to the benefit of village councils (recruited on the basis of individual qualities) and associations (in which there is competition between 'grades'); these positions are obtained only after fierce competition.

This typology is more descriptive than classificatory. As Eisenstadt admits, it is based on a limited sample; it cannot be placed at a sufficiently abstract level and offers therefore only quasi-models. Lastly, it is not homogeneous, a fact which is revealed by the single domination of each of the types. The resistance of political systems to formalization appears, once again, in the limitations of this attempt. In the case of the segmentary societies, the reduction of the political to the structures governed by descent and alliance ignores certain of its most specific aspects, while the search for the political 'outside kinship' seems to yield poor results. Power and 'kinship' are in dialectical relation, hence the failure of any unilateral interpretation.

Chapter Four

Social Stratification and Power

Political power organizes legitimate domination and subordination and creates its own hierarchy. Above all, it gives 'official' expression to a more fundamental inequality: that of the social stratification and system of social classes established between individuals and groups. The mode of differentiating between the social elements, the various orders within which they exist and the form taken by political action are closely related phenomena. This relation emerges as a fact – in the historical development of political societies – and as a logical necessity – power results from dissymmetries affecting social relations, while these relations create the differential 'distance' necessary to the functioning of society.

All societies, in varying degrees, are heterogeneous; history adds new elements to them without eliminating all the old ones; the differentiation of functions multiplies the groups that carry out these functions or makes the same group take on different 'aspects' according to the situation. These various elements may be adjusted only if they are ordered in relation to each other. Politics unifies them by imposing an order and it has been said, with good reason, that it is 'the ordering force *par excellence*' (Freund). In short, there are no societies without political power and no power without hierarchies and unequal relations between individuals and social groups. Political anthropology must neither deny nor ignore this fact; on the contrary, its task is to reveal the particular forms adopted by political power *and* the inequalities on which it relies in the so-called 'exotic' societies.

Those societies possessing only a minimal government, or which reveal it only in a circumstantial manner, are no less bound by this obligation. Power, influence and prestige result

from conditions that are now better known, such as the relation
with ancestors, the holding of land and material wealth, the control over the men who can be put into battle against external
enemies, the manipulation of symbols and ritual. These practices already imply antagonisms, struggle and conflict. These
societies possess elementary social hierarchies, united between
themselves by a dialectic that foreshadows 'the elementary
forms of the class struggle' (R. Bastide) in the more complex
societies governed by the primitive state.

1. Order and Subordination

Anthropological theories appear to be marked by uncertainty:
some of them see the expression of relations of hierarchy and
domination in 'nature' – either in the 'pecking-order' of bird
societies or in the situation of the 'dominant males' in groups of
monkeys; other theories, however, ignore the formal aspect of
the relation and see social stratification as 'rooted in culture'
(Fallers). It is linked to an ideal image of man that symbolizes
the collective values and ideals and classifies individuals and
social groups by reference to this model. From this point of view,
hierarchization represents the passage from nature to culture
and this change should be more perceptible in the simpler
societies.

The debate, even when reduced to this summary formulation,
suggests the ambiguities that obscure the notion of social
stratification. Contradictions remain as to the nature of the inequalities that should be taken into account when characterizing
this stratification. The so-called 'natural' inequalities, based on
differences of sex and age, but 'treated' by the cultural environment in which they are expressed, are revealed in a hierarchy of
individual positions placing men in relation to women, and each
individual within the sex group according to age. In an article
published in 1940, Ralph Linton draws attention to this 'aspect
of social organization'. He contrasts the Tanala of Madagascar,

who possess a double hierarchization of men and women according to age and to proximity to the ancestors, and the Comanche Indians, who also possess a double hierarchization, which places at the summit men at the peak of their virility and women at the peak of their fertility. In the first case, the hierarchy is continually ascending and continues into the world of the ancestors; in the second case, it is first ascending, then descending. The predominance of religious values among the Tanala and of military values among the Comanche helps to explain this difference, and shows that the natural criteria of 'classification' derive their meaning from the culture that uses them.

These primary inequalities already determine privileges and obligations. They become more complicated when they intervene in the field of relations defined by kinship and descent.* Moreover, their relation to the political changes according to whether they determine the respective positions of individuals or those of social groups. Kinship determines the first in particular, although its structures reveal 'classes' of kinsmen and the play of equality (for example, between brothers) or of domination–subordination (for example, between parents and their children). It operates within a small framework in which it establishes authority relations linked to a system of titles, attitudes, rights and obligations. Nevertheless, it assumes political significance only in so far as it influences the relations between social groups and between individuals, and also in so far as it regulates accession to the posts conferring power and authority. The social units formed by descent are not all equal and equivalent, but operate within a hierarchical order of groups and involve unequal statuses (even if the inequality concerns only prestige and pre-eminence) and an unequal share in the exercise of power. The dominant principle on which this order is based is that of seniority and genealogical proximity: the descent group 'closest' to the common ancestor or founder occupies a superior position, possesses political pre-eminence and attributes power to the oldest member of the oldest generation.

*Cf. Chapter 3, 'Kinship and Power'.

This hierarchy may be justly regarded as foreshadowing the elementary forms of social stratification. It is a product of history and justifies itself by reference to myth – the founding ancestors being regarded as gods or heroes, or at least as their companions. The relative position of the clans and lineages results from the events that led to their formation, from the initial stratum, and their progressive occupation of space, from the spot where the foundation took place. Thus, among the Bemba of Zambia, the clan lineage order takes its reference from Atimukulu: 'his' lineage has a monopoly of political power and 'his' clan (that of the crocodile) has the highest status by virtue of its antecedence; the other clans and lineages are placed according to whether their founder arrived with or after the conquering hero. In societies with a traditional state the same principles may still operate. Among the Swazi of southern Africa, the first king known to oral tradition founded the leading clan from which the sovereigns are recruited, and the lineages forming this clan are hierarchized according to their relation to the primordial line. History has affected the hierarchy of clans and lineages, brought out differences of 'rank' within the clan system and affected the organization of social space.

History often begins with a mythology that expresses inequality of status symbolically and provides a justification of the domination–subordination relations that this involves. This function of myth is clearly apparent in certain Amerindian societies. Thus the mythology of the Winnebago of Wisconsin relates how two 'halves', one 'heavenly' (the possessor of ritual powers), the other 'earthly' (the possessor of the techniques necessary for material subsistence) fought, in the beginning of time, over which of them would occupy the post of chief. The first won and established his domination: one of the clans that formed this 'half', that of the Thunderbird, has a monopoly of the tribal chieftainship. The bipartite organization of the Winnebago tribe is based on this inequality of status and political power. 'Those from above' are of a higher rank, occupy the 'right' part of the tribal territory and their clans have birds as their totemic emblems. 'Those of the earth' are inferior in status, occupy the 'left' part of the tribal territory and their class have earth-bound animals as totemic emblems. They intervene in the political sphere only in a secondary way, by exercising, for example, the functions of the police (the bear clan) and the office of public crier (the bison clan). They remain outside real political power, which strives to conform to the designs of the 'supernatural powers'.

It has been said that the hierarchy of individuals in a kinship system and the hierarchy of 'segments' in a segmentary society obey the same principles of ranking. In fact, this is merely an approximation that blurs the political implications of the second of these orders. It would be just as risky to proceed in the same way and regard the implications of the criterion of age as similar within a kinship or lineal system and within a system of age-group hierarchies. In his book *From Generation to Generation* (1956), Eisenstadt has justly observed that the institution of age groups cuts across the boundaries of kinship and descent, introduces a new mode of solidarity and subordination and goes beyond the particularisms of lineal groups. By giving yet another support to primitive political power and by enabling more 'universal' values to prevail over 'particularist' values, it sometimes operates in contradiction with the system of social relations based on kinship and descent, notably in societies in which a pre-eminent age-group (that of the warriors) imposes celibacy and a minimal participation in the kinship structure on its members. Such is the case of the Meru of East Africa.

The stratification of age-groups differs from a mere hierarchy of generations. It results from both age *and* the ritual procedure that conditions access to the system, creates a sort of school of civics and confers adult status. The organization of age-*groups* sets up relations of solidarity and also of authority – modified perhaps by a play of compensations – which links the relations of domination between successive 'groups' (1–2) and the free relations between alternate 'groups' (1–3), as is the case in several societies of the southern Cameroons. However, the essential character of *instituted* age-groups is to establish a social stratification outside kinship and descent and to facilitate the performance of specific functions – ritual, military, and/or political.

It is in Black Africa that this system shows the greatest diversity of form (cf. Eisenstadt, 1954). The Nandi and Kikuyu-Kamba of East Africa possess a social organization based on territory, a hierarchy of age-groups with military, political and juridical responsibilities that intervenes *directly* in the government of the collectivity, while clans and lineages are reduced to a secondary role. In West Africa, for example among the Ibo of Nigeria and their neighbours, age-groups are one of the basic elements of the village structure; they have an economic function and can decide participation in the running of village affairs. Southern Africa, with the Swazi and Zulu kingdoms, shows how a strongly centralized power rests on a powerful age-group structure: these groups form regiments, bound to the sovereign, which play more than a military role. These examples do not give an adequate notion of the many variations on the age-group theme to be found in African societies. A more detailed comparative study would show that the ordered age-groups occupy different positions in society as a whole according to whether the clan/lineage hierarchies are still active, and according to whether the strictly political stratifications are constituted or not. Their position, structure and functions change in consequence: it is between these two poles – a merely segmentary society/a society with a traditional state – that they are invested with the more numerous or more important functions, including those of government.

These *elementary* forms of social stratification, involving clans or lineage and age-groups, are never abolished. They usually co-exist with more complex forms that dominate and use them, by means of variable procedure. According to some anthropologists, including G. P. Murdock, these forms alone can really be called 'stratification'. According to Murdock, the term can be applied only to societies in which *essentially* distinct

and unequal groups appear – unequal by virtue of their difference: for example, those that involve a distinction between free
men and slaves. The pertinent criterion then becomes the
inequality of status or position expressed outside *kinship* and
outside the relations established between descent-groups and age-
groups. The social statuses concerned, the ranks and orders they
govern, result from relations foreign to the spheres in which
these three models of relations operate, and are based on conquest, the control of land, ritual ability, the establishment of
slavery, etc. These complex stratifications are expressed in unequal (or exclusive) shares in the exercise of power, wealth and
prestige symbols, and by cultural differences. They may foreshadow a social class structure; they do reveal very clearly the
effects of history.

Ethnological literature provides a great many examples, from
different parts of the world, of this type of society possessing
ranks, orders or castes. It is to be found among the North
American Indians – the Indians of the North-West and the
Natchez of the lower Mississippi valley. The Natchez distinguish between the common people – called rather unflatteringly
the 'stinking' – and the aristocrats, who are themselves hierarchized into three categories, 'honourables', 'nobles' and 'suns'.
The supreme chief, situated and isolated at the summit of this
hierarchy, was given the title of 'Great Sun'. However, this
system of ranks remained open to the play of marriage and merit
(Swanton, 1911). In Polynesia, social distinctions are more
marked. Thus, in Samoa, multiple levels are established and
ordered even outside the dominant distinction between free
men and the others. J. B. Stair (1897) distinguishes five 'classes'
of free men, each with its internal hierarchy: the political 'class'
(the chiefs, who are far from equal among themselves), the
religious 'class' (the priests), the landed nobility, the great landowners and the common people. Some of the responsibilities
and some of the titles are hereditary. In a comparative study,
M. D. Sahlins (1958) has shown the diversity of the forms of
stratification, their degree of unequal complexity in Polynesian

societies, and has tried to relate them to the insular ecologies and economies, and to the types of political structure and organization.

Africa offers a great variety of societies with complex social stratifications. Some have an overall 'caste' system, hierarchizing a small number of enclosed, strictly differentiated, specialized and essentially unequal groups. This is the case of traditional Rwanda and Burundi; in Maquet's phrase the 'premise of inequality' is the principle on which the domination and privileges of the superior, minority group is based. Certain societies, notably in Senegal and Mali, combine a system of orders (aristocrats, free men, slaves) and a system of professional 'castes', each with its own stratification and specific hierarchy. The Wolof and the Serer, the Tukulor, belong to this category. Some other societies, such as the Hausa of northern Nigeria, combine in a totality of 'extreme complexity' (M. G. Smith) multiple modes of stratification and hierarchization. In this case, the structure can be explained by ethnic heterogeneity, the high degree of differentiation in the economic and social functions and the frequency of conquest practised by a group that has obtained a monopoly of power. The *traditional* African societies that appear to be formed by proto-classes or embryonic social classes are rare; the kingdom of Buganda, because of the place accorded to landed property and the importance given to individual initiative, seems to be one of these. It is not without interest to mention that Ganda society is one of the traditional societies most open today to the process of modernization, especially in the political field.

Asia, with India, offers the greatest number of caste societies. The cohesion of these societies is a result neither of the family structure (which has been called 'centrifugal'), nor of the clan system (which has been called 'nominal'), but of caste. It establishes a strict order, differentiation and specialization, erects frontiers that accentuate the differences by preventing the encroachment of one group on another and organizes a division of space that conforms to these requirements. This mode of social

relations and the inequalities it brings with it are explained
and justified by reference to the religious system and to ritual behaviour. The model of the four *varnas* (basic classificatory categories) is the instrument that makes the *theoretical* interpretation
of this total arrangement possible. The reality is much more
complex, for it varies according to region and period. Moreover,
the multiplication of castes and their internal divisions causes a
permanent controversy as to their relative positions. Endogamy
can operate at every level of the internal stratification, as in the
case of the Brahmins of Bengal* (Hsu, 1963). The dynamism of
the castes is linked to political dynamisms, and it was an over-
simplification if the castes were at first defined in terms of an
unchanging system. Most Asiatic societies possess complex
social stratifications, of which the Kachin of Burma, studied by
Leach, are an illustration. He sees their society as a combination
of a 'class system' and a 'lineal system' in the process of being
transformed, not without difficulty, into a 'feudal system'. He
distinguishes three main orders or 'estates' and two intermediary
ones:

1. that of the chiefs or lords (*du*);
2. that of free men (*darat*);
3. that of the 'slaves' (*mayam*);

between 1. and 2. are the aristocrats, the presumed descendants
of former chief; between 2. and 3., the descendants of a *darat*
man and a *mayam* woman (the *surawng*). This stratification is
neither rigid nor in direct correlation with economic status. It
relates to ritual distinctions and political considerations. It
enables each order to exalt its 'honour' in regard to those inferior to it. But the essential fact is no doubt that it is rooted in
the field of relations defined by kinship, descent and alliance. In
a way, it seems to be a superior, systematized expression of
inequalities existing at this level.

This brief, incomplete account of the various complex

*L. Dumont (1966) has emphasized the ideological aspects of the caste
system.

stratifications and hierarchies reveals the multiplicity of their traditional forms; it also suggests the difficulty of trying to reduce this multiplicity to a limited number of types. The differentiation between the superior forms and the elementary forms of the stratification is not an easy one to make, for in a sense the first spring from the second, and use them when expressing a change of hierarchical regime. The controversies of the specialists lead at last to the question of their respective frontiers. However, it would appear legitimate to confine the application of the concept of stratification to societies which satisfy at least two conditions: (1) the dominant inequalities are formulated on the basis of other criteria than those of age and sex, kinship and descent; (2) the distinctions established between hierarchized groups are drawn at the level of the society as a whole or of the national political unit. But this definition hardly simplifies things, for the passage from theoretical interpretation to the elucidation of social reality is not without difficulty. Concrete societies appear as 'a tangle of social stratification systems in dialectical relation with each other'. This definition by R. Bastide (1965) echoes that of G. Gurvitch which identifies 'every structure' with 'a precarious balance, which must be constantly re-established by sustained effort, between a multiplicity of hierarchies'. Moreover, the effective relation linking social stratification to political structure and organization is established according to variable modalities; it is neither simple nor unilateral – and research conducted under cover of political anthropology should not ignore this fact.

2. Forms of Social Stratification and Power

Before analysing this relation we should first examine the concepts most commonly used in their connexion – they are also the most problematic. The critical inventory worked out by Lowie in the chapter 'Social Strata' of his *Social Organization* (1948a) would suggest this. The notion of *status*, inherited from

Maine and Herbert Spencer and taken up by modern sociologists and social anthropologists, defines the personal position of an individual in relation to others within the same group; it makes it possible to appreciate the social distance between people, because it governs hierarchies of individuals. *Role* expresses status in terms of social action and represents its dynamic aspect. Both notions, linked to a collection of rights and duties, must be legitimized, either by custom, or by a specific procedure or ritual. The notion of *office*, which is linked to the first two, implies them both and may be regarded as a generic term of which they would be particular cases. It denotes the function occupied by virtue of a 'mandate from society', determines the type of power or authority conferred within the framework of political, economic, religious or other kinds of organization and draws a distinction between the function itself and the individual who holds it for a time.

Office necessarily entails ceremonial and ritual elements which, by 'a deliberate and solemn procedure', effect the accession of its holder and invest him with a 'new social identity'. A complex relation is established between the office and its holder: if the first remained vacant, the social order would appear to be threatened; if the second did not conform to the obligations and prohibitions imposed by the office, but accepted only the privileges that it brings with it, there would be the same risk. Office not only has a technical aspect; it also has a moral and/or religious character that is obviously accentuated in the case of politico-ritual functions. Fortes says of these functions: 'Their religious character is a way of investing with binding force the moral obligations to society, for its well-being and prosperity, which those who accept office must solicitously translate into actions' (1962, p. 83).

Certain offices are linked to a 'received' status which, by virtue of descent, age or the possession of some native quality, is attributed to only a small number of persons. Others may be open to every member of society, or be the privilege of particular groups – as when a title remains the exclusive property of a certain lineage. In most traditional centralized societies political offices are reserved to members of 'a ruling class that represents only a small proportion of the total population' (Peter C. Lloyd).* It may correspond to an ethnic entity that has unified a plural society and imposed its domination, or to a descent group that occupies pride of place in a totality of ordered clans or lineages, or to a hereditary aristocracy that possesses a culture distinct from that of the majority.

In every case the notion of office denotes the notions of *rank* and *order* or *estate*. It expresses political power, and its own hierarchy, in its relation to social stratification. The terms rank and order (or estate) are often confused, or used interchangeably, in anthropological literature; and it is true that these concepts overlap to a large extent. The first, however, refers to a particular hierarchy, either that of social groups based on descent, socio-professional groups or offices within the political organization. The second, following the usage established by historians, refers to a total hierarchy: that presented by every society in which there exist almost closed, *legally defined* classes, for which membership is governed basically by the fact of birth. The system of orders or estates must be seen as one of the complex forms of social stratification, parallel to the caste system and to the class system.

These two systems remain at the centre of a debate the details of which cannot be gone into here. Certain authors (including Rivers) apply the term 'caste' only to the Indian phenomenon. They lay down four criteria for its fulfilment: endogamy, hereditary function, strict hierarchization and rules of 'untouchability'. Other authors (including Lowie) try to give it a wider application. They reject the distinction drawn between caste and class and propose a continuum of hierarchized classes, within which castes are characterized only by their 'extreme fixity'. This, according to Lowie, makes it possible to differentiate within the same society between the less 'permeable' strata

*Cf. his study in the A.S.A. symposium, M. Banton (ed.), *Political Systems and the Distribution of Power*, London, 1965.

(castes) and the more 'permeable' (classes). If one accepts this interpretation – and the differential value it confers on the criterion of 'permeability' or openness – castes, orders (or estates) and classes appear as three elements in a progression towards a more open hierarchy of social groups. According to this interpretation, clan societies or age groups performing specific functions contain within themselves the germs of these three complex forms of social stratification.

The controversy has flared up once more on the basis of observations collected by anthropologists in recent decades. The Indian castes now appear to be less 'closed' and also less fixed than the classical definition implied; Hsu recalls that the system has always incorporated new caste groups and that the breakdowns and struggles affecting the system are not only modern phenomena. Moreover, societies outside India possess a partial stratification comparable with that regulated by castes. African examples have already been proposed: these show the link between orders and castes within the same political unit (the Wolof, Serer and Tukulor of Senegal). Scientific prudence leads one to see systems of castes, orders and classes as 'ideal types' that never exactly coincide with reality and which may be used in conjunction in any exploration of this reality. It is of the utmost importance to be quite clear that the first two are in some way related and that the third occupies a place apart. Castes and orders on the one hand and social classes on the other are contrasted in the same way as 'imposed' groups are to 'factual' groups, dominant function groups (political, ritual, economic, etc.) to supra-functional groups, groups in complementary relation with groups in an antagonistic relation. These three 'cardinal criteria', among the six used by Gurvitch (1954) to define class, make it possible to reveal the differences. If, on the other hand, one regards castes, orders and social classes as the three modes of a hierarchical combination established between men, symbols and things, one sees that the first refer above all to the symbolic sphere par excellence, religion, the second to those supposedly innate attributes that make men unequal and the third to things from the point of view of their production and distribution.

The interpretation of traditional societies in terms of social classes is unusual in anthropology, for reasons that primarily concern the facts and only secondarily the orientations of the research. Even the Marxist theory seems incomplete, or hesitant, in this sphere; it sees a transition from a classless society (the primitive community) to a class society, but without treating the problem in its entirety and without explaining in detail why pre-capitalist social structures require a more 'complicated' interpretation. It is Georg Lukacs, in his *History and Class Consciousness*, who uses this term and introduces a useful warning: in the case of these structures, 'it is by no means certain that one can differentiate the economic forces from other forces'; in order to 'discover the role of the motive forces of society, one needs more complicated and much more refined analyses'. Most Soviet ethnographers, using the model of development worked out by Engels, link the existence of the traditional State to unequal social groups that may be regarded as *proto-classes*, one of which exerts domination and exploits the others. The use of the notion of proto-classes at least suggests the difficulties: it shows how necessary it is to distinguish it from the concept of class as developed in the critical study of nineteenth-century European capitalist society. Non-Marxist anthropologists assume an even greater distance between the two. Thus, Fallers affirms that the notion of social class, which is 'distinctive' to western history and culture, is unusable outside societies formed by that history and culture since it has not been given 'a significance of general application'. The work of anthropologists, and of sociologists considering traditional non-European societies, reveals the existence, under the influence of decolonization and modernization, of incipient rather than fully formed classes. They link this structural change to more recent developments.

The question of the validity of the concept of social classes, applied to a field that is not its original field, is still an open one.

It is legitimate to apply it only to unified societies (which implies the presence of a state) in which the 'economic forces' determine the predominant social stratification, and in which antagonistic relations threaten the established social order and political regime. But it should be recognized at once that very few of the societies that are the subjects of anthropological research come into such a category. Certain recent studies attempt to identify, within these societies, the class relations and 'antagonistic interests' that they give rise to. In his study of traditional Rwanda, Maquet (1964) makes just such an attempt: he recognizes the existence of 'an economic relation between the two strata' (the Tutsi and the Hutu) which makes it possible 'to consider them as authentic social classes'. And it is true that events – the 1960 'revolution' that overthrew the monarchy and Tutsi domination – seem to confirm this new analysis. Moreover, research has been devoted to the ideological expressions derived from relations of inequality and from the modes of distributing political power, and to expressions of contestation and rebellion. L. de Heusch has shown how, in the case of Rwanda, a rejection of the existing state of things may be expressed at the level of myth and religious innovation: an egalitarian cult (the *Kuban-dwa*), which sprang from the Hutu peasantry, opposes an imaginary society to the real society based on inequality (Heusch, 1964). Gluckman has devoted himself to the analysis of the political dynamic (power struggles) and forms of rebellion (reactions operating against the holders of power). But above all he has tried to show that these forms of rebellion have the effect of consolidating the political regime, rather than altering it, either because they remain contained within the framework of ritual, or because they are aimed against the holders of political office and not the system.

This new direction has made some initial progress. It is striving to seize the internal dynamic of systems of social stratification – which is a necessary, if inadequate condition, as soon as one tries to apply the concept of classes to some of the societies studied by anthropologists. The field of accepted, and sometimes routine, preoccupations – study of the 'subcultures' associated with the various strata, examination of the means used to defend occupied rank or to legitimize social ascent, study of the matrimonial processes that make it possible, through endogamy, hypergamy or differential marriage, to maintain a significant gap between the hierarchized social groups, etc. – is thus widened. Further progress will be made when economic anthropology is more developed – for it will lead to a more acute and more diversified knowledge of the 'modes of production' proper to 'traditional' societies – and when the theoretical contribution of political anthropology is enriched. The bases of inequality and the organization of power that this inequality necessitates will then appear with greater clarity – and be more favourable to detailed analysis. The verification of correlations will gain in rigour: between castes and weak power operating within a system defined by its 'centrifugal characteristics', to use Hsu's term, between orders (or estates) and strong power that appears to be linked to a closed recruitment and to a defence against contestation and, lastly, between proto-classes and an effective power characterized by greater openness and a greater sensitivity to contestation and change.

Before verifying this relation between social stratification and the types of political power we must create the instrument that will enable us to analyse complex and overlapping 'group hierarchies'. A single example is enough to show how necessary this is – that of the Hausa of northern Nigeria. The simplistic dualism that contrasts the aristocrats and the common people (*talakawa*) in that society fails to take into account a situation resulting from a great many historical vicissitudes. It is, in fact, a relatively recent society in its present form (early nineteenth century), founded on conquest, established on highly differentiated ethnic entities, in which the state was set up by force and in which the social and political hierarchies are interlinked. Nevertheless, the offices (*sarautu*) associated with the royal power confer more in the way of prestige and privilege, and constitute in a way the hierarchy of reference. Subjacent to the system are the inequalities set up between ethnic groups and the elementary inequalities established according to sex, age and position in the kinship and descent groups. The function performed determines a hierarchical order, which confers status and rank on each individual: at the summit, the aristocrats with a monopoly of the political posts; at the base, the butchers who form the most discredited group – the eleventh. Each group has an internal, more or less formalized hierarchy and personal success (*arziki*) leads to a kind of promotion. Relations between widely separated groups are almost non-existent, except in the case of authority relations; social relations between close groups are active and are often expressed in the form of 'playful kinship' (*wasa*). This ordered arrangement of socio-professional groups is placed within a hierarchy of orders or estates: (1) aristocrats; (2) worthies and Islamic scholars; (3) freemen; (4) serfs and domestic slaves. The political and administrative organization determines a hierarchy of status, rank and office that dominates the whole, which, in turn, is established according to status (royal lineage being obviously placed at the top), and according to the office held (certain slaves attain posts as civil or military functionaries). The principal relations, between the various systems of inequality and subordination, may be depicted in the following form.

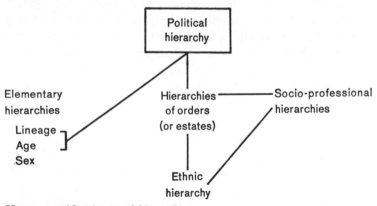

Hausa stratifications and hierarchies

The simplicity of this table should not conceal the complexity of Hausa stratifications, for it takes no account of the distinctions of rank and hierarchy within these stratifications. It would have been further complicated if we had added the relations of 'clientage' (client: *bara*), which are of a more contractual nature and which create a network of ties between socially and politically unequal persons. This, then, gives some idea of the need for a detailed analysis in the case of societies that place political power within multiple and interlinked hierarchies.

3. 'Feudality' and Relations of Dependence

The studies made by anthropologists of what they call 'feudal' societies provide concrete evidence of the articulation of a system of inequalities and of a political regime, despite the controversy concerning the comparability of the true feudalities – those of the European Middle Ages – and the pseudo-feudalities that have existed, and still exist, in Asia and Africa. Mention of this controversy, which has been based above all on recent work in Africa, is necessary, for it has made possible a better understanding of the social and political relations that *together* characterize feudality. For Maquet, feudality 'is not a mode of production' (although it requires a surplus of consumer goods), but 'a political regime', 'a way of defining the roles of government and governed'. The specific fact is the interpersonal link: 'Feudal institutions set up between two persons unequal in power relations of protection on the one hand and of fidelity and service on the other.' They link the lord with the vassal (at the higher level of social stratification) and the patron with the client (from a higher to a lower level of stratification). Maquet (1961) finds in this the 'universal content of the idea of feudality', the distinctive feature that makes it possible to erect it into the 'ideal type', in the sense used by Max Weber.

For Lucy Mair, the relation of personal dependence (clientage)

is above all one of the means of political competition, even
if it has provided 'the germ from which state power springs'
(1962). The feudal analogy hardly enters her analysis. Authors
like Jack Goody (1963) and John Beattie (1964) carry the controversy farther. Goody recalls that the term feudality may be
used in two senses: a general sense that defines 'the dominant
forms of political and social organization during certain centuries of the European Middle Ages' and a more specific sense
whose necessary criteria are the relation of dependence (lord/
vassal) and the existence of fief – the basis of this relation. A
comparison may be made at the first level, but it remains an
approximate one of little scientific use. At the second level, the
deviance of the African 'feudalities' is very apparent; the personal link is not the result of a decline of the state, but, on the
contrary, of a process culminating in the organization of a centralized power; fief does not acquire the permanent character
that it had in Europe from the end of the eleventh century, for
it remains precarious and tied to a political or administrative
function, the holder of which changes according to the wishes of
the sovereign or when a new reign begins.

Beattie also draws a distinction in referring to the definition
of feudality formulated by Marc Bloch (1949) and in applying
the 'feudal model' to the particular case of Bunyoro (Uganda).
He shows that the existence of about a dozen 'great territorial
chiefs' does not in any way affect the central position of the
king, the *mukama*. All power and all authority proceed from him
and he delegates them according to a ritualized procedure,
transmits them as rights over a particular territory and over a
peasantry that is confined to that territory, in exchange for
service – of an essentially military nature until colonization.
Similarly, the king is linked to the people as a whole through a
mystic identification and the play of institutions. He is dissociated from the aristocratic clan, he is surrounded by representatives of all the clans and all the trade guilds and he is at the
centre of the system of exchanges, in turn receiving and giving.
In Bunyoro, the network of 'feudal' relations does not come

between the sovereign, the chiefs of the various orders and the subjects, but is, in fact, 'the means of sustaining a system of centralized administration'.

Recent analyses of monarchical Rwanda and of Burundi have also modified the image of African feudalism (Lemarchand, 1966; Troubworst, 1962). Lemarchand observes that the first is reminiscent, in its political system, of the feudality of Japan and not that of medieval Europe. Social stratifications, the hierarchies of power and authority and interpersonal relations are in correlation with 'a complex of rights and privileges' based on ownership of land and cattle. *Local* political life is based on 'three major institutions': lineage, headship and the 'fidelity' group organized around a 'patron'. It reveals a society that is not really unified, but which, on the contrary, combines very different social and political relations; relations regarded as feudal are only one of these constitutive wholes – they serve as a base for a political organization that remains threatened by the strength of the powers and rights of lineage. Troubworst presents a reinterpretation of Rundi society that corrects earlier accounts. He shows that a monopoly of power is in the hands of a small aristocracy; the true governors are 'the princes of the blood royal', and relations of 'clientage' operate above all within the dominant caste (that of the Tutsi), where they provide an instrument of social promotion. They are based either on cattle, in which case they are private in character and easily revocable, or on land, in which case they necessarily have a political significance, create a circle of favourites and clients and are linked with the 'politico-territorial hierarchies'. But the dominant fact, in Burundi, is the close connexion between a social stratification that transcends the 'caste' system and participation in political power. The holders of territorial authority are both the most powerful and the richest; they have a 'monopoly of control over goods'. The 'feudal' relationship intervenes as a means placed at the service of a strategy whose aim is conservation, by a small aristocracy and its dependents, of power and possession. This example reveals a new mode of African feudalism; it suggests its variations and, by contrast, its frequent instability. In Asia, this instability has been remarked on, notably by Leach who has revealed the 'difficult transition' of Kachin society* towards a clearly constituted feudal-type system.

*A traditional society in Burma.

Chapter Five

Religion and Power

Sovereigns are the kinsmen, the homologues or the mediators of the gods. The closeness of the attributes of power and of the sacred indicates the link that has always existed between them – a connexion that history has tended to pull apart but has never broken. The work of historians and anthropologists on the superior powers associated with the royal person, the rituals and ceremonial of investiture, the procedures that maintain a certain distance between the king and his subjects and, lastly, the expression of legitimacy provide overwhelming evidence of the indestructibility of such a link. But this link is best expressed in times of new beginnings, in periods when kingship emerges from magic and religion, in the veiled form of a mythology that constitutes the only 'account' of these events and affirms the double dependence of men established by gods and kings. The sacrality of power is also expressed in the feelings that bind the subject to the sovereign – a veneration or total submission that cannot be justified by reason, a fear of disobedience that has the character of a sacrilegious transgression.

The presence of the king-god, the king by divine right or the king-thaumaturge, is not a necessary condition of the recognition of this link between power and the sacred. In societies of the clan type, ancestor-worship or the worship of gods specific to the clan is generally a guarantee of the sacralization of a still undifferentiated political sphere. The lineage or clan 'chief' is the point of contact between the real clan (or lineage), formed by the living, and the idealized clan (or lineage), the repository of ultimate values, symbolized by the totality of the ancestors: it is he who transmits the words of the ancestors to the living and those of the living to the ancestors. The overlapping of the sacred and the political is already, in such cases, incontestable. In modern secularized societies, it is still evident; power is never completely emptied of its religious content, which is reduced, inconspicuous, but none the less present. If, when civil society was established, the state and the church were originally one, as Herbert Spencer claims in his *Principles of Sociology*, the state always preserves some of the characteristics of the church, even at the end of a long process of secularization. It is the nature of power to maintain, either in an overt or in a masked form, a political religion. This fact explains Luc de Heusch's brilliant, and apparently paradoxical, formula; 'Political science derives from the comparative history of religions' (1962).

In this respect the political philosophy of Marx foreshadows the work of sociologists and anthropologists, for whom it provides a point of departure by showing the presence, in every society possessing a state, of a dualism similar to the opposition of the sacred and the profane: 'The members of the political state are religious by virtue of the dualism between the individual life and the generic life, between the life of the civil society and political life.' Marx analyses the nature of the transcendence proper to the state and reveals how it is imbued with religious feeling. According to Marx, state power and religion are similar in their essence, even when the state is separated from the church and in opposition to it. This essential similarity is due to the fact that the state is situated (or appears to be) beyond real life, in a sphere whose distance is reminiscent of that of God or of the gods. It triumphs over civil society in the same way as religion conquers the profane world. These initial observations must be complemented, and verified, by a more far-reaching elucidation of the sacred nature of politics than is possible within the scope of anthropology alone.

1. The Sacred Bases of Power

The relation of power to society is – as I have already emphasized – similar to the relation that, according to Durkheim, exists between the Australian totem and the clan. This relation is essentially imbued with sacrality, for every society links its own order to an order beyond itself, and, in the case of traditional societies, to the cosmos. Power is sacrality because every society affirms its desire to be eternal and fears a return to chaos as the realization of its own death.

a. Order and disorder

But the work of political anthropology insists not so much on the needs of a particular order, as formulated by the society, as on the principal means used by that order: the legitimate use of physical constraint. Political anthropology suggests – as de Heusch has remarked – that 'every government, every *sovereign*, is to a varying degree ... both the depository of constraining physical force and a priest of the cult of Force'. A rigorous analysis must consider these first two fundamental ideas together; on the one hand, the sacrilization of an order that is shown to be necessary to security, prosperity and survival; on the other, the recourse to force, which makes it possible to order, in the full sense of the term, and serves as an expression of the vigour of power.

An examination of 'indigenous' theories of power shows that it is often seen as being linked to a force regarded as its very substance, or as its condition as a force of subordination, or, again, as the proof of its legitimacy. By emphasizing the ambivalence, or ambiguity, of this force, such theories reflect the specificity of the political. They recognize the capacity of this force to act on men and on things in a good or a bad way according to the use to which it is put; they see it as the instrument of command, but they also point out that it dominates whoever holds it; they link it not so much to the mortal person of the sovereign as to a function that is declared to be eternal. The struggle for power confirms the indigenous theory and is primarily a struggle to win control of the instruments that fix and canalize the power force itself.

Research conducted in Africa in the last two decades has helped us to understand this manifestation of power. It shows that the notions that serve to qualify the substance of power belong not only to the political vocabulary, but also to religious language, and all reflect the sphere of the sacred or exceptional. Thus the theory of kingship developed by the Nyoro of Uganda involves the concept of *mahano*, a power that enables the sovereign to maintain the appropriate order and which is transmitted, right down through the politico-administrative hierarchy, according to a strict ritual procedure. *Mahano*, however, intervenes not only in the political field. Beattie has shown that it is associated with a number of different situations that must possess at least one characteristic in common. It is recognized in the irruption of strange or disturbing events and in the manifestation of violence: it expresses, therefore, an external threat. As soon as social behaviour infringes the fundamental prohibitions, those on which the principal social relations are based, such as relations within the clan, relations of kinship and of fictitious kinship (established by the blood pact) or the relations regulating status, according to sex, age or rank, *mahano* becomes present and active. In this second case, *mahano* reveals dangers that society bears within itself. Lastly, it intervenes in the course of individual lives at birth, initiation and death – that is, at the times of the 'passages' that bring into play the vital forces and the 'spirits' that control them. It can be seen, then, that whether in the relation of the society to its universe, of Nyoro man to his society, or the individual to the powers that govern his destiny, *mahano* is always present. It expresses a relation of subordination and reveals a distance that enables the vital flow to circulate and order to prevail. It might be said that the political apparatus is the regulator of *mahano*: the positions of power and authority that it defines are justified by the unequal access of their holders to the force that maintains life and order.

For his subjects and his country, the Nyoro sovereign is the supreme vessel of *mahano*. The many rituals that form and protect the royal person as the symbol of life also defend society against death. The king is he who dominates people and things and maintains their order. Through him, the constraint of the order of the world and that of the social order are imposed conjointly. It is his hold on *mahano*, on the dynamisms that constitute the universe and society, that enables him to assume his functions. This hold is, in itself, a source of danger, for power imposes its own law on whoever possesses it, otherwise it operates wrongly and destroys what it is intended to preserve. The notion of *mahano* expresses this deadly risk in terms of pairs of antagonistic notions: order/disorder, fertility/sterility, life/death. The dialectic of command and obedience appears, then, as the expression, in the language of societies, of a more essential dialectic – *that possessed by any living system in order to exist.* It is the possibility of being, and of being together, that men revere through their gods and kings.*

An examination of the African concepts that express power and its substance reveals certain common aspects – the most important ones – and certain significant variations, for they are as diversified as the political systems to which they refer. For the Alur of Uganda, who have created chiefdoms that have imposed their domination on neighbours devoid of any differentiated power, the notion of *ker* is one of the principal elements of political theory. It denotes the quality of being chief, the 'power' that enables its holder to exert a beneficial domination, and which is so necessary that the peoples who do not hold it must hope to receive it from the Alur. It is not materialized and remains quite distinct from the office and material symbols associated with the chiefdom. It presents a quantitative aspect, being

*For information concerning the Nyoro, cf. the studies of J. H. M. Beattie (1959b; 1960a; 1960b).

an organizing and fertilizing force that can lose its intensity – in which case, it is said that 'the *ker* is cooling down' or that 'the tooth of the chiefdom is becoming cold'. Three factors determine the vigour of its intervention in the service of men: continuity (for the *ker* retains its 'heat' by being maintained in a long line of descent), the personality of its user and the conformity of the relations established with the sacred. This last condition is of some importance. The Alur chiefs act as privileged mediators between their subjects and the 'supernatural powers', for they are linked both to their personal ancestors *and* to the ancestors that make up the history of the chiefdom. They show their ability to govern by the ritual mastery they exert over nature – they are recognized as 'rain makers' – and, in a certain way, it is their control over the vital forces and over things that justifies their control over men. The chiefs control their subjects, but the power controls those who are its depositaries because its source is situated in the sphere of the sacred. It establishes itself as an ordering factor, while entropy threatens the social system, and acts as a guarantee of permanence, while death carries off the generations and those who govern them (cf. Southall, 1956).

Two examples from West Africa confirm the scientific interest and importance of an analysis devoted to the terminology of power as presented by indigenous theory. One of these was mentioned in an earlier chapter, that of the Tiv, a large people of Nigeria, in whose society government has remained 'diffused'. In this case, power is seen in terms of two opposed and complementary notions, one entirely beneficent (an order that ensures peace and prosperity) and the other dangerous (a superiority acquired at the expense of others). In its most elaborated version the political theory is formulated in the language of religion and witchcraft. All legitimate power requires the possession of *swem*, an ability to be in harmony with the essence of creation and to maintain its order; more broadly, this term denotes the ideas of truth, well-being and harmony. The *swem* is also a force that cannot act without a support, or an intermediary, whose own quality conditions the consequences of this intervention for human affairs: a weak link brings about a general lack of energy while an abusive link becomes a cause of disorder. None the less, the word *swem* denotes power in its essentially positive aspect. Inversely, the second notion (*tsav*) governs the domination over beings, material success and ambition. When it denotes ability based on talent and individual enterprise – whether of the renowned chief, the influential elder or the rich man – it is regarded as favourable; but it also qualifies the successes obtained at the expense of others, the constraints exerted over them and the inequalities that exploit the 'substance' of inferiors – and in this sense it is associated with witchcraft and the counter-society. Tiv theory emphasizes the ambiguity of power and the ambivalence of the attitudes towards it that lead to its being accepted as the guarantee of an order propitious to human activity (it expresses the will of the gods), while feared as the instrument of domination and privilege, since its depositaries may constantly overstep the tolerable limits.

The second example is that of a huge, very ancient and highly organized society, that of the Mossi of the Upper Volta, whose sovereign (*Mogho Naba*) symbolizes the universe and the Mossi people. The key-concept, as far as politics is concerned, is that of *nam*, which refers to the power of earlier days – to that employed by the founders in the building up of the state – and to the force received from God 'which enables a man to dominate others'. Its dual origin, divine and historical, makes it a sacred power that confers on the group that holds it supremacy (a 'noble status') and the ability to govern. Although the *nam* is the condition of all power and all authority, it is never acquired permanently. Its possession is the object of political struggle: failure brings its loss, as well as the abandonment of power and prestige. This notion primarily concerns legitimate domination and the struggle for the positions from which it can be exercised.

The term *nam* belongs to a wider complex of meanings. It applies to absolute superiority: that of God, that of the king, that of the political order that dominates the structure of social relations. It justifies the privileges associated with superior social positions: the right to claim wealth, services, women and the symbols of prestige. It expresses the necessity of power as a defence against the dangers of deculturation and of a return to chaos; this explains why the king and chiefs must 'eat the *nam*' if disorder is not to 'eat' the works of men. In its most complete and sacralized form the *nam* is an assurance of legitimacy, for it testifies that the power received emanates from royal ancestors and that it will operate in a manner that conforms with the well-being of the Mossi people. It is fixed in the regalia, and in the sacred symbols associated with the person of the sovereign – the *namtibo* – and is communicated through these to the ritual drink that links the king with his ancestors and to the divinized Earth, the chief to his own ancestors and to the *Mogho Naba*. To 'drink the *namtibo*' is to receive the *nam* and to be bound by an oath of obedience, of submission to the order inherited from the founders of the kingdom and to the orders that emanate from the man who is their legitimate successor.*

According to Paul Valéry, the politician acts on men in a way that is reminiscent of 'natural causes'; they submit to him as they submit to 'the caprices of the sky, the sea and the earth's crust' (*Regards sur le monde actuel*). This analogy suggests the distance from which power emanates – outside and above society – and the extent of its constraining force. The four political theories just sketched confirm this interpretation, as well as indicating its limits. They show power as a force, associated with the forces that govern the universe and preserve life, and also as a power of domination. They associate the order of the world, imposed by the gods, with the order of society, established by the early ancestors and founders of the state. Ritual ensures the preservation of the first and political action of the second: *they are regarded as related processes.* They both help to impose conformity on a total order that is presented as the condition of all life and all social existence. This identification of the sacred and the political, which means that opposition

---

*A description of the system and of the political representations proper to the Mossi is to be found in the work of E. P. Skinner (1964).

to power (but not to its holders) is sacrilegious, takes on different forms according to the political system; in the case of 'stateless' societies the sacred is of primary importance, while in societies with a highly organized state greater emphasis is placed on the domination exerted over men and things. Moreover, the theoretical elements considered here show power in its dynamic aspects: it is a force for order, an agent in the struggle against factors of change, which are associated with witchcraft and deculturation; it confers a power that is acquired through competition and which must be preserved. In most African kingships periods of interregnum impose a controlled disorder that arouses a desire for the restoration of power and a confrontation between the rival claimants that makes it possible to select the most vigorous of them. Lastly, the underlying notions of political theory show the ambivalence of power: it must exert a beneficent hold on the basic dynamisms of the universe and of society, but there is also a risk that it may be distorted into a force that is ill-controlled or used beyond the limits required for legitimate domination.

This method of analysis would be applicable to the so-called archaic political societies that have been studied outside Africa if the information required had been collected in sufficient quantity. In fact, the description of the political organizations and political functioning has received more attention from research workers than has the study of the political vocabulary and the theories of the human groups being 'interrogated'. The necessary data may sometimes be found, significantly enough, in the study of religious forms. This would therefore (and also) suggest that the relation of political power to society is similar to that between the sacred and the profane; in both cases the chief good appears as order and its opposite as chaos.

In societies whose attitude to nature is less conditioned by a desire to dominate it and who see it both as their own extension and reflection, the link between the sacred and the political is particularly strong. Both categories may be defined in parallel – the principles and relations they imply 'correspond' with each other. Both presuppose distance or break, either in relation to the profane sphere, or in relation to civil society, the sphere of the 'governed'. Both refer to a system of prohibitions or orders, to formulas, which, like the Greek *themis*, assure the ordering of the world and of society. Both are profoundly ambiguous. The sacred and the political are concerned with complementary and antithetical forces whose *concordia discors* is a factor of organization, and are thus based on a dual polarity: that of the pure and the impure, that of the 'organizing' (and just) power and the 'violent' (and constraining or contesting) power. They are both associated with the same symbolic geography; the pure is linked to the 'within', the centre, and the impure to the 'without', to the periphery; similarly, the beneficent power is situated at the very heart of the society of which it is the focus, while the threatening power remains diffused and, for this reason, operates rather like witchcraft. R. Caillois (1939) qualifies this opposition by the words 'cohesion' and 'dissolution'; the first refers to the powers that 'preside over cosmic harmony', which 'preserve material prosperity and good government' and defend 'the integrity of man's physical being' – they are incarnated in the sovereign; the second refers to the forces that provoke disturbances, anomalies and transgressions affecting the political or religious order – they are expressed through the witch-doctor. Lastly, it should be remembered that the two categories of the sacred and the political are linked to the ability to act effectively, to a power of intervention or action, as denoted by such terms as *mana* in the sacred vocabulary and such terms as *mahano* or *nam* (considered above) in the political vocabulary. The two series of notions interlock. The forces or substances to which they refer arouse the same contradictory feelings: respect and fear, attraction and repulsion.

The homology of the sacred and the political is such that these two concepts are regulated by a third notion that dominates them both: that of order, or *ordo rerum*, whose importance has been pointed out by Mauss. In 'archaic' societies the elements of the world and the various social categories obey the same classification models. Their ordering, which is regarded as being subject to the same laws, is expressed in a dualist form: * it reveals a bipartition of the organized universe (the cosmos) and of society, and concerns antithetical and complementary principles, whose opposition and association result in the creation of an order, a living totality. This 'order of things', or of 'men', results then from the separation *and* the union of the two series of elements or opposed social groups: the natural elements, the seasons, the cardinal points, on the one hand; the sexes, the generations, the phratries, on the other. Correspondences are established between the opposed series of categories. The dominant characteristic of this mode of representation is the necessity of establishing a break between the 'classes' thus constituted *and* of assuring a union between them. The separation of contraries makes order possible, their union establishes it and makes it fruitful. This elementary dialectic governs the initial interpretation of nature and of the society that can result from this 'sociological homosexuality' realized by the alliance of homologous groups.

The notions of the sacred and the political are part of this system of representations, as their parallelism suggests. In the case of so-called complex societies, possessing hierarchies and clearly differentiated authorities, the relations between political power and religion are not radically altered. Beyond the hierarchized, unequal groups, with their 'oriented' relations (of domination and subordination), there is postulated a relation of complementariness between the sovereign and the people, between the governors and the governed. The relation established between the king and *each* of his subjects is regulated by the principle of authority, opposition to which is equivalent to a sacrilege; the relation established between the king and the totality of his subjects is seen in terms of the complementary dualism. It is reminiscent of a formula of ancient China. 'The prince is *yang*, the multitude *yin*.' The sacred and the political together contribute to the preservation of the established order;

* Cf. the classical study by E. Durkheim and M. Mauss (1901–2).

their respective dialectics are similar to that which constitutes that order – and together they reflect that which is proper to any system, real or theoretical. What men revere through the guardians of the sacred and the depositaries of power is the possibility of constituting an organized totality, a culture and a society.

b. Entropy and renewal of order

The *ordo rerum* and *ordo hominum* are threatened by entropy, by the destructive forces they bear within themselves and by the wearing out of the mechanisms that maintain them. All societies, even those that appear to be least subject to change are obsessed by the feeling of their vulnerability. A recent work devoted to the Dogon of Mali shows, on the basis of an analysis of the 'theory of the word' and of the system of representations, how this society, by means of force, assures the struggle against destruction and the continual conversion of imbalance into balance, while appearing to be in conformity with the primordial model (Calame-Griaule, 1965).

Beyond their multiplicity, the processes of re-creation and renewal possess one common characteristic; they operate both on the social universe and on nature, their actors are both men and their gods. By causing the irruption of the sacred and by re-establishing in disturbance and abundance a kind of original chaos, which serves as a return to the moment of first creation, the festival appears as one of the most complete of these acts of renewal. There are, in fact, a number of processes that contribute, in a more or less obvious, more or less dramatized, way to this task of permanent recreation. One less schematic, less static interpretation of the 'archaic' societies makes this apparent. In an article devoted to a new appreciation of the data of 'New Caledonian Sociology', P. Métais emphasizes the importance of Kanaka marriage in this respect; its ceremonial causes a rejuvenation of social relations – society appears to be recreated when a marriage union and the new alliances it brings about are created (Métais, 1961).

The rituals and teaching prescribed by initiation, which conditions access to 'fullness' and to full 'citizenship', usually have the same aim; society restores its own structures, and the order of the world within which it exists, by opening the way for a new generation. In the ancient kingdom of Kongo, the initiation procedure known as *Kimpasi* is particularly concerned with this function, all the more so in that it operates at times when the community is weakened or threatened. The community tries to assure its safety by reliving its own youth, that is, the period that saw the collective enterprise that shaped its order, its culture and its history – for the specific rites form a symbolic return to the age of creation and beginnings. Society rediscovers its earlier vigour by re-enacting its own genesis. It assures its own rebirth by bringing to birth, according to its own norms, the young men fashioned by initiation (cf. Balandier, 1965b).

To the very extent that death is regarded as a manifestation of disorder and scandal, the funeral ceremonial is also a means of restoration and recovery; it reveals, through its participants, the basic social relations; it establishes an intense relation with the sacred; it leads, when the period of mourning is over, to a purification and a new alliance with the community of ancestors. The intensity of the struggle against the process of dissolution can be appreciated more precisely if one remembers that witchcraft – although regarded as the absolute nonconformity, a form of invidious warfare, the manifestation of the counter-society – may be converted into a means of reinforcement. The collectivity isolates its evil by designating its aggressor, the sorcerer or the radical opponent, and claims to be re-establishing itself by neutralizing him. In his study of the Kachin of Burma, Leach compares the functioning of witchcraft with the 'mechanism of the scapegoat'.

The mechanisms of recreating order necessarily involve the holders of power, and therefore some of these mechanisms help to maintain the political machine. This is apparent when Lowie, considering 'some aspects of the political organization' of the Amerindians, discovers the religious basis of power, the co-operation between the chiefs and the specialists in the super-natural and the relation between the chiefs and the seasonal events (such as harvests) that link the social and the natural orders. In Melanesia, the facts speak with even greater clarity. The New Caledonian chief imposes his authority by the power of his speech – it is he who *orders*, in every sense of the term – and who holds, in Guiart's words, a 'quasi-cosmic responsibil-ity'. His effective participation in the cultivation cycles is ex-plained by this obligation; it forms a kind of link between the renewal of nature and the strengthening of men. It is on the occasion of the most important and most *total* of the rituals – that of the *pilu-pilu* – that the new chief, who presides over it, is 'revealed to all' and affirms his authority through 'the skill of his speech' and his ability to follow the course of the prescribed words. This social ceremony involves the community in its en-tirety: it seeks to propitiate its ancestors; it honours the dead and marks the end of mourning; it exalts new births and assures the 'entry of the initiated young men into full manhood'; it confers on each category of participants a particular station and includes a distribution of goods, according to an order based on 'the political past' and the relations established by it. Lastly, it combines in a magnificent spectacle, in which dancing expresses the dynamism of the universe and society, men, their ancestors and their gods, their wealth and their symbolic riches.* This ceremonial provides a perfect expression of the basic social rela-tions, including antagonistic relations, which are converted into 'games of opposition'. By offering to the eye a sort of résumé of society as a whole, it makes it possible to capture an *enacted* social system, corresponding to its theoretical formulation, embodied through the means of expression proper to a society without a written language: symbolic behaviour, specific dances and speeches that followed a significant convention. It has a therapeutic effect: it releases the community from its potential

*For a detailed description, cf. M. Leenhardt (1930).

conflicts and tightens the links between clans separated by great distances. In these moments when the society becomes fully conscious of itself and of the universe with which it is in harmony, the chief appears as a central figure. It is around him, and by means of a sort of challenge to the outside world, that the cluster of social forces is reformed. This renewal operates periodically, three years at least separating the ceremonies, for they require a massive accumulation of riches. The cycle of the festivals coincides with the cycle of revitalization, which enables the chief not to be opposed and to remain in the eyes of all *oro kau*, the 'great son'.

c. Return to the beginnings and ritual rebellions

The struggle against entropy may assume a more directly political character. In traditional societies possessing a monarchical state, each change of reign brings about a return to the 'beginnings'. The accession of the new king is an occasion of repeating symbolically the creative enterprise of kingship, the acts of foundation that established and legitimized it. The investiture evokes – through the procedures or ritual that embody it – the conquests, the exploits and the magical or religious acts that are said to constitute royal power. Georges Dumézil was one of the first to suggest this, in connexion with the Roman kingship. He shows how the succession of the 'first kings of Rome' formed a sequence in which two 'royal types' alternated. Though received from a tradition older than Rome itself, these types are none the less presented as the creators of the city. The reigns of the immediate successors of Romulus and Numa reproduce, by alternating them according to a determined order, the creative violence and *celeritas* of the first and the organizing wisdom and *gravitas* of the second. They therefore obey a dualistic theory of power and put into action the means that make it possible to re-invigorate it by a kind of return to its distant sources.*

*Cf. in particular G. Dumézil (1943).

The process appears most clearly in the case of African kingships based on 'magical polarity', to use de Heusch's term. On
his accession to power the king is bound to perform a sacred act,
which, while recalling the act of foundation, qualifies him as
king. Either by performing some heroic exploit that shows him
to be worthy of his office and demonstrates the victory of the
royal 'party' over the ambitions of feudal factions, or by showing
the negation of the old social order and the establishment of the
new order, the protection of which is invested in the state, by an
act of rupture (incest), the sovereign becomes a person who no
longer belongs to the common order of men (cf. de Heusch,
1959, 1962). The procedure of investiture involves the same
attempt at reinforcement. Thus, in the ancient kingdom of
Kongo, it establishes a symbolic return to origins, by means of
a ceremonial that associates the new king, the elders and the
people and invokes the founding partners: the descendent of the
founder and the representatives of the ancient occupants of the
region that corresponds to the royal province, who have become
the 'allies' of the Kongo kings. It invokes the spirits of the first
kings, 'the twelve generations' to which they are associated, and
necessitates the handling of the most ancient symbols and insignia. It returns to the time of a history that has become myth
and reveals the sovereign as the 'forger' and guardian of Kongo
unity. The enthronement of the king assures not only the legitimacy of the power held, but also the rejuvenation of the kingship. It gives the people (for a time) the feeling of a new beginning (Balandier, 1965, part 2, chapter 4).

A similar reinforcement of rule and power, associated with
an affirmation of the necessity and innocence of the function of
sovereignty, is apparent in the practice of 'acts in reverse' and in
the recourse to rituals of inversion or dramatized rebellion. The
history of Antiquity reveals a very ancient use of these mechanisms. The Greek Kronia and the Roman Saturnalia both involved an overthrow of the relations of authority that acted as
a regeneration of the social order. Like Rome, Babylon made use
of a mock king and inverted positions of rank during the feast of

the Saceae. On the same occasion, a slave who had played the role of the king, giving orders, using the sovereign's concubines and abandoning himself to orgies and sensual gratification, was hanged or crucified. This unleashed power is *a false power*, an instigator of disorder, not a creator of order; it arouses a desire for the return of the reign of law.

Modern anthropologists have re-examined these procedures, which tend to purify the social system by mastering the forces of dissolution and periodically revitalize political power. In his collection of earlier papers, Max Gluckman (1963) offers some illustrations from Africa. They are all the more significant in that they refer to states that are unstable on account of their technological backwardness and lack of 'internal economic differentiation'. Among the Swazi, an annual, national cere-mony, the *incwala*, links the ritual of inversion to the collective action required during the first harvests. It involves two phases. The first submits the capital to a symbolic sacking and the king to expressions of hatred – sacred songs affirm that his 'enemy', the people, have rejected him. However, the king emerges strengthened from these trials; he becomes once more the Bull, the Lion, the Indomitable. The second phase begins with the eating of the first fruits; it is led by the sovereign and follows an order of precedence that expresses the various social statuses and the hierarchies that they determine. The social order is thus exposed and is renewed at the very moment when the ties with nature and the cosmos are tightened. The sovereign remains both an object of admiration and love and an object of hate and repulsion; he pretends to be unwilling to resume his place at the head of the nation, then finally yields to the demands of the members of the royal clan and to the solicitations of his warriors. Power is then restored, unity recreated and the identification of king and people re-established. The *incwala* ritually frees the forces of contestation and transforms them into factors of unity, security and prosperity. It imposes the social order as a replica of the order of the world and shows them to be necessarily linked, for every break entails the risk of a return to chaos.

Research recently conducted in the Ivory Coast, among the Agni of Ndenye, has brought to light a ritual of social inversion (*Be di murua*) that takes place during periods of interregnum. During such a period the relations between free men and court captives are reversed. As soon as the king is dead, the captives take possession of the royal enclosure and one of them – the captive-king – seizes all the insignia of power; he establishes a temporary court and hierarchy; he occupies the seat of the dead sovereign and enjoys all the royal prerogatives; he demands presents and can order his men to seize the provisions stored in the capital. Everything takes place as if society became a caricature of itself as soon as the supreme power was left vacant, and governors and governed exchanged roles. The captive-king proclaims the vigour of his command over men and of his domination 'over the world'; the free men submit to this royal simulacrum, knowing that a regent is discreetly running affairs and preparing the accession of a new sovereign. The outrageous behaviour of the captives is expressive of their precarious elevation – the disappearance of the king breaks their dependence – and contrasts with the constraints or prohibitions imposed on the free men by the royal mourning. They put on the richest loin-cloths; they make merry and order large quantities of drink; they claim to have rediscovered their rights and status. They violate the most sacred commandments. In inverting the civil and political society of which the sovereign is the guardian, they can replace him only by a mock-king, an aberrant order, a system of false rules. They show in a certain sense that there is no alternative to the established social order but derision and the threat of chaos. The day the dead king is buried the false power is abolished, the captives tear up their silk loin-cloths and the captive-king is put to death. Each subject and each thing resumes its rank and place and the new sovereign can assume the direction of an ordered society and an organized universe (Perrot, 1967). Contestation in ritual form belongs therefore to the strategy that enables power periodically to give itself a new vigour.

2. Strategy of the Sacred and Strategy of Power

The sacred is one dimension of the political sphere; religion may be an instrument of power, an assurance of its legitimacy, one of the means used in political struggle. In his work on the religion of the Lugbara of Uganda, Middleton (1960) is essentially concerned with the relation between 'ritual' and 'authority'. He shows that the ritual structures and the structures of authority are closely linked, that their respective dynamisms are in correspondence. In this lineage-oriented society ancestor worship serves as the basis of power; the elders use it in order to contain the claims to independence of their juniors; the conflicts between the generations (differentiated by unequal status) are mainly expressed in mystical and ritual terms. Lugbara patrilineages are defined genealogically *and* ritually: they are both descent groups and groups of people linked with the ancestral spirit. The elders at their head justify their power and privileges as much by their access to the altars of the ancestors as by their genealogical position – so much so that 'a man who can successfully invoke the dead may be accepted as the true elder' (Middleton, 1960, p. 12). The strategy of the sacred, when directed to political ends, appears under two apparently contradictory aspects; it may be put to the service of the existing social order and its acquired positions, or serve the ambitions of those who wish to conquer authority and legitimize it. Political struggle uses the language of the invocation of spirits and also that of witchcraft; the first is the weapon of those holding power; the second the instrument of those who contest them and see their weaknesses and abuses as the work of witch-doctors. The Lugbara are very aware of this manipulation of the sacred and their ritual contradictions express the contradictions of their real life. Middleton provides a striking description of the relations thus established between the various agents of political strategy: 'God, the dead and the witches enter into the system of authority, as well as living men' (1960, pp. 23–4).

Fortes reaches a very similar conclusion from his research among the Tallensi of Ghana. He shows that ancestor worship must be interpreted in this classic society not so much by reference to a metaphysic and an ethic as by reference to the system of social relations and to the politico-juridical system: 'The Tallensi have an ancestor cult not because they fear the dead – for they do not, in fact, do so – nor because they believe in the immortality of the soul – for they have no such notion – but because their social structure demands it' (Fortes, 1959, p. 66). This necessity takes the form of a privileged relation established between the ancestors, who are invested with supernatural power and are beneficiaries of a cult, and those living men who possess a superior social status and a share in political power. In fact, not all the dead become ancestors, but only those who have left a 'depositary', an heir who assumes their office, their prerogatives and a share of their possessions. Men of inferior social status, who have only an undifferentiated and mediated relation with the ancestors as a whole, are contrasted with those of superior status who have a specific and direct relation with certain ancestors. The political strategy is organized on the basis of this ritual relation. The eminent dead, who have been given the status of ancestors, and the eminent living, who hold office and power, are linked closely together. The first are 'omnipotent'; the submission that they require 'on pain of death' assures the placing of the individual within a determined social order. They are the basis of the power of those who are their depositaries within society, and all new power can only be established in relation to them.

The relations established between political power and the sacred are as clearly apparent at the level of mythology. Malinowski suggested as much in considering myth as 'a social charter', as an instrument manipulated by the holders of 'power, privilege and property' (1936). In this respect myths have a dual function: they *explain* the existing order in historical terms and they *justify* it by providing it with a moral basis and by presenting it as a system based on right. Those myths that confirm the dominant position of a group are obviously the most significant; they help to maintain a superior situation. Monica Hunter Wilson emphasizes this use of myth in relation to the Sotho and Nyakyusa of southern Africa. They claim to have brought fire, cultivated plants and cattle into the region where they settled and declare that they owe their monopoly of political power to their civilizing mission; they claim to possess, in their very being, a vital force that they are able to transmit to the country as a whole. The ceremonial and ritual of the succession to the chiefdom recall these claims in a symbolic fashion; the myth is then made present once more in order to renew and reinforce the political power (Wilson, 1960). In a more theoretical study, Audrey Richards examines the 'mechanisms' of maintaining and transferring 'political rights' – that is, the procedures and strategies that make it possible to keep power, privileges and prestige – and remarks that they imply a reference to a more or less mythical past, to acts of foundation, to a tradition. The various versions of the myth assume the appearances of history and the incompatibilities express real contradictions and con-testations; they express, in their own language, the struggles of which the political rights are the object (Richards, 1960).

In societies with a centralized state, the mythical knowledge (the 'charter') is often held by a body of specialists whose work is secret; it is no more shared than are the political functions themselves. The *bakabilo*, of the Bemba of Zambia, are the ex-clusive guardians of the mythico-historical traditions and the hereditary priests of the cults necessary to the correct function-ing of the monarchy. They are agents of conservatism and lend a mask of tradition to inevitable changes. In traditional Rwanda, privileged royal councillors – the *abiiru* – hold the 'esoteric code of the dynasty'. They must supervise the application of all the rules concerning the institution of the monarchy and the sym-bolic behaviour of the king. Their function is both political and sacred. They make sure that the prescriptions imposed on the sovereigns are respected and also modify the 'code' in order to adapt it to new circumstances and to legitimize changes that contradict the constitutional canons. It is through their mediation that the sacred intervenes in the play of the strategies of power.

It should not be concluded from these examples that political power possesses a total mastery of the sacred and can turn it to its own use in all circumstances. In Austro-Melanesia, where the chiefdoms are superimposed on an earlier political structure, the bipartition of responsibilities – action on men, action on the gods – shows the ritual limits of power. In his structural study of the Melanesian chiefdom, Guiart elucidates the principles that govern the division of 'tasks' between the chief (*orokau*) and the master of the soil (*kavu*); the first acts through the word, or command; the second acts through the rituals that are the instruments of the *ordo rerum*. The contradiction that exists between these two partners constitutes a good deal of the dynamism of society; it shows that the strategies of power and of the sacred are not always identical. Consequently, attempts at strengthening traditional kingships often lead to an extension of their control over religion. Thus, when 'African despotism' assumed its definitive form among the Ba-Ganda of Uganda, the control of the clan cults (which honour the ancestral spirits known as *lubalé*) was tightened. These cults, which are not exclusive of other practices, seem to be both specialized and hierarchized. The *lubalé* revered by the sovereigns occupy pride of place and have a national status, for they control war and material power, fecundity and fertility. Moreover, the sovereigns have at their disposal royal *lubalé* that operate uniquely to the benefit of the reigning king; they also enforce the transfer to the outskirts of the capital of the altars devoted to the clan cults and thus bring them under control just as they are trying to reduce the power of the clan chiefs. Having failed to establish a single national religion, the Ganda kings have concentrated on their ability to intervene in the sphere of the sacred.

The strategy of the sacred also serves to limit and to challenge political power, but in a contrary way. In a study concerning 'the abuses of political power', Beattie differentiates between

the 'categorical' aspects (and norms) and the 'conditional'
aspects (and norms). The first have a permanent, one might say
constitutional character, the second appear only in certain conditions, when the established procedures can no longer operate
effectively; in all cases, it is a question of preventing governments and their agents from acting in a way that is not in conformity with the conception of the office that they hold. The
rituals of enthronement and the oaths that they impose, the
refusal of ritual collaboration operating against the sovereign
and the abdications required for reasons of ritual weakness are
some of the sacred means that make it possible to contain the
supreme power or to challenge abusive rulers.

The instrument of religion can also be used for a more radical
contestation. In situations of crisis, prophetic and Messianic
movements reveal the weakness of the existing order and the
rise of rival powers. In his analysis of the political organization
of the 'American aborigines', Lowie remarks on this when he
shows that the power of the Amerindian chiefs has always
weakened when confronted by that of 'messiahs'. He observes
that these messiahs are not so much the agents of a reaction
against the intrusion of strangers as the providers of the confidence and hope desired by a threatened and degraded society.
In Melanesia and Black Africa the decline of the traditional
chiefs during the colonial period has encouraged the rise of men
who propagate new cults, creators of indigenous churches who
offer a renewed social framework and the model of a revived
state. Religious conflicts are a clear expression of political
struggle – which they provide with a language and means of
action – in situations caused by the weakness of the established
power.

Religious innovation can lead to a refusal that finds a solution
on an imaginary level or to opposition and even rebellion. In
traditional Rwanda, in East Africa, the autocratic government of
the sovereign and the basic inequality that maintained the privileges of the aristocracy brought about both reactions. The initia-
tory cult of *Kubandwa*, which developed among the peasantry,

substituted an immense fraternal family of initiates for the real society. Against the historical king who dominated his subjects by his despotic rule it set up a mythical king who ruled over the spirits known as *Imandwa*. It saw this mythical king as a saviour who acted for the good of all his adepts without the discrimination of social status. It established a mystical equality beyond the subordinations of real life. In the felicitous phrase of de Heusch it banished the existing profane order and introduced 'the phantom of a better order'. The second cult of contestation appeared later, about the middle of the last century. It was addressed to *Nyabingi*, a woman without femininity, a kinglike servant who had died and whose return was awaited. She would return to deliver the Hutu peasants from the servitude imposed on them by the Tutsi aristocrats and to free their 'priests' from persecution. She exercised a kind of kingship at a distance, and the guardians of her cult held real power, which set them in opposition to the delegates of the Rwandese sovereign. She was responsible, then, for the setting up of a counter-society: episodic revolts took place in her name and revealed a nostalgia for the old social order that had existed prior to the Tutsi domination. Her cult illustrates one of the primitive forms of social movement which, throughout its pre-history and its pre-revolutionary history, has constantly turned the sacred against those who monopolized it in order to consolidate their power and privileges (cf. Hobsbawm, 1959).

Chapter Six

Aspects of the Traditional State

Having once enjoyed the almost exclusive attention of political thinkers, the state now seems to have fallen into neglect. Indeed, so advanced is this process of decline that the recent thesis by G. Bergeron (1965), in which he offers a theory of the state, concludes that such a theory is not 'a major theoretical concept'. The state is now regarded, according to the definition of Freund (1965), as 'one of the possible historical conformations by which a collectivity affirms its political unity and fulfills its destiny'. This definition is itself derived from Max Weber, who reduces the state to one of the 'historical manifestations' of the political – the one that characterized above all the development of the political societies of Europe from the sixteenth century and which culminated in the formation of the modern state.

Wider interpretations of the state, identifying it with any autonomous political organization, are on the decline,* while the analysis of the political phenomenon is now quite distinct from the theory of the state, whose heuristic value diminished long before the real object that it claimed to interpret underwent such radical changes. This development can be explained in part by the progress of anthropology, which involves the recognition of 'other' political forms, and the diversification of political science, which has been forced to interpret the new aspects of political society in the socialist countries and in the ex-colonial countries. Specialists have been forced, for reasons that concern both developments in knowledge and changes in the facts themselves, to shift the centre of their preoccupations; and those who have succeeded in doing so are no longer fascinated by 'the institution of institutions: the state'. Some ten

* Cf., as an illustration of this point of view, W. Koppers.

years ago, Easton expressed this change in condemning definitions of the political sphere that took cognizance only of the
state. Such definitions lead, in fact, to the more or less explicit
statement that no political life existed before the appearance of
the modern state; they are directed towards the study of *a*
certain form of political organization and fail to examine the
specificity of the political phenomenon; they encourage im-
precision to the extent that the state remains a general framework
for ill-defined contours (Easton, 1953). The debate is still open.
Political anthropology can offer its own contribution by trying
to determine rigorously the conditions that it imposes on the
use of the concept of the state in the case of certain of the
societies it considers and by re-examining with greater precision
the problem of the origin, characteristics and forms of the primitive state. By doing so, it will return – but with new information
and new scientific methods – to certain of the preoccupations
that caused it to emerge.

1. The Questioning of the Concept of the State

The widest interpretations see the state as an attribute of all
social life, a mode of social arrangement that operates as soon as
the state of culture is established, a necessity proceeding from
'the very essence of human nature'. It is identified, then, with
the means used to create and maintain order within the limits
of a socially determined area: it is 'incarnated in the local
group' (Koppers, 1963). This point of view is held above all by
conservative theoreticians who wish to exalt the state *while
depriving it of its historical aspect*. Thus, for Bonald, the state is a
primitive reality, the instrument by which *every* society ensures
its own government. According to a similar interpretation – a
distant heir of the political thought of Aristotle – the state is
identified with the widest group, the superior social unit, the
organization of society as a whole. The historian E. Meyer
(1912) offers a definition of this kind: 'The dominant form of the

social group, which contains within its essence the consciousness of a complete unit, resting on itself, we call the state'.
The criteria for identifying the state are therefore its totalizing
character, its autonomy and its power of domination. Faced
with the difficulties resulting from the use of the concept of the
state in a wide sense, jurists have been led to restrict its use and
to define the state as the system of practised juridical norms.
They qualify it as a juridical phenomenon and emphasize that
it has realized, to a very high degree, the institutionalization of
power. This is a false interpretation, for it reduces the state to
its 'official' aspects and does not situate the problems at their
true level, which is primarily political.

Between these two positions – one loose, the other restrictive
– are the more usual definitions. They characterize the state
by three main aspects: the reference to a spatial framework, to a
territory; the consent of the population(s) living within these
frontiers; the existence of more or less complex organic structures on which the political unit is based. These criteria are no
longer really specific; they are to be found in attempts to cir-
cumscribe the political sphere;* they are applied to the most
varied political societies; they involve too wide a use of the
notion of the state. Such hesitations and uncertainties are very
revealing and they show how difficult it is to conceive of a non-
state political organization, even in the case of 'tribal' societies.
Attempts have been made to define precisely at least one type
of reference: that of the modern state, developed in Europe,
which seems to serve as a model to the developing political
societies. Freund, for example, uses 'Max Weber's ideal type
method'. He reveals three characteristics:

1. the first, already accentuated by the German sociologist,
is the rigorous distinction between the external and the internal: it governs intransigence in sovereignty;
2. the second is the enclosure of the State political unit:

* Cf. Chapter 2, 'The Political Sphere'.

it defines a 'closed society' in Weber's sense, occupying a clearly demarcated area;

3. the last is the total appropriation of political power: it requires opposition to all forms of power of private origin.

This construction of the ideal type of the modern state does not eliminate the difficulties, for the first of these characteristics is applicable to all forms of the political unit, while the other two may arguably describe certain 'traditional' states. Moreover, Freund is led to emphasize a criterion regarded as preponderant, namely, the rationality of the state. This criterion enables him to contrast 'instinctive' (whether tribal or urban) political creations and the 'improvised' political structures produced by conquest (empires or kingdoms) with the state, which is 'the work of reason'. This does not preclude the recognition, however, that every state construction is the product of the progressive rationalization of an existing political structure (Freund, 1965, pp. 560 ff.).

The problems of the sociology of the state have usually been abandoned before being resolved or even properly presented. Thus, the interpretation outlined above culminates only in a conception of the state as an image and realization of reason, inspired by the political philosophy of Hegel. This gives rise to a question: do the political philosophers suggest answers that the sociologists and anthropologists have so far failed to provide? It is all the more necessary to consider this question in that the contribution of the political philosophers has often been rejected on account of the normative preoccupations, beliefs and assertions that underlie their theories. The confrontation cannot be merely avoided – it would become derisory; on the contrary, it should be shown to be necessary and scientifically effective. Thus a comparison of Hegel's commentaries on the pagan state and the theories of the traditional state enunciated by certain anthropologists – including the Africanist Max Gluckman – would reveal some significant similarities. In both the accent is placed on the ethnic basis of the ancient state, on the internal contradictions between the sexes, between kinship (in the widest sense) and the state organism, and on the essentially non-revolutionary character of the state, which, in this case, is associated with a 'world' and a society considered to be in dynamic equilibrium.

Before evaluating the contribution of political anthropology, a few remarks on sociological theories of the state should be made. Marx shows that the state is neither the emanation of a transcendent rationality, nor the expression of an immanent rationality within society. He presents, under different aspects, the relation between the state and society, while constantly maintaining a critical spirit.

1. The state is identified with the organization of society; the affirmation is quite unambiguous: 'The state is the organization of society.'

2. The state is the 'official expression' of society; in his correspondence Marx remarks: 'Take any civil society and you will have a political state that is only the official expression of the civil society.'

3. The state is a fragment of society erected over it; it is a product of a society that has reached a certain stage of development.

These definitions are neither equivalent, complementary, nor perfectly compatible. The problem seems to have been eluded if one holds to the third, most vulgarized interpretation, on which Engels based his theory of the state:

'Society creates an organism with a view to the defence of its common interests against internal and external attacks. This organism is the state power. It is no sooner born than it makes itself independent of society, all the more so in that it becomes more and more the organism of a certain class and that it works directly for the domination of that class.' *

The political sociology of Proudhon also contains a critical theory of the state – and one so radical that it is transformed into

*In *Ludwig Feuerbach and the End of German Classical Philosophy.*

total opposition to all political systems that merely maintain respect for state authority. Proudhon denounces the common error by which the state is accorded a specific reality possessing in itself its own power. In fact, the state proceeds from social life. Expressing and instituting a social relation of hierarchy and inequality, it emanates from society, appropriating its power, while remaining outside it, and achieving a monopoly of the 'collective force'. The relation of the political to society is compared with that between capital and labour: social life and the centralized state are necessarily in a relation of radical contradiction, as the diagram below makes clear:

Social life $\longrightarrow$	Exchanges	Law of reciprocity
State $\longrightarrow$	Authority Constraint	Non-reciprocity

Even more than on the constitutive inequalities of the state, Proudhon insists on the oppositions between society and the state: those of the multiple (social life is characterized by the plurality of inter-group relations) and the unitary (the state tends to reinforce its own unity), the spontaneous and the mechanical, the changing and the fixed, creation and repetition (cf. Ansart, 1967). The first of these oppositions is based on Proudhon's belief in 'decentralization' or 'political federation'. It also suggests the permanent debate, which has been thoroughly examined by political anthropologists, that takes place within *every* society between the segmentary and the unitary. Proudhon's theory of the political emphasizes certain requirements of method: the need to understand the movement by which society creates a state, to grasp the relation of the state with society as a whole, to see it as the official (and symbolic) expression of society and as the instrument for preserving established inequalities.

Durkheim observes that the state results from the division of social work, from the transformation of the forms of solidarity, and tries to show that the state is only one of the historical guises assumed by the political society. Indeed, he is at great pains to distinguish between the two: the state is an organism that has become pre-eminent among the social groups that make up the political society. It is a specialized group, the holder of sovereign authority, the place where decisions concerning the whole collectivity are taken. This interpretation culminates in a conception of the state that might be called mystical. Using metaphorical language, Durkheim characterizes the state by its ability to 'think' and to 'act' and sees it as the agent of social thought. He also confers on it a function as the protector against the risks of despotism in society, for the secondary groups may be held in check by the state and vice versa, while with the broadening of its field of action there is an increase in the liberty and dignity of individuals. Durkheim, then, owes nothing to earlier critical theories, and by 'a curiously abstract and intellectualized conception', to use L. Coser's words, he gives substance to the state, while ignoring the coercion it exerts and the ambiguity of its relations to society (cf. Durkheim, 1893, 1950). Although he identifies the development of the state with the movement of rationalization with which modern civilization is credited, Max Weber pays less attention to the historical structure of the state than to the interpretation of the political phenomenon in general. He emphasizes one of the characteristics concealed by Durkheim's analysis: the state is an instrument of domination, a group with a monopoly of legitimate physical constraint – and having at its disposal an apparatus, including the army, which exists for this purpose; like every domination group, it confers on a minority the means of deciding and directing the general activity of society. In this sense, the state is encouraged to intervene in every sphere, which, with a 'rational' administration at its disposal, it can do. In a way, it is defined as the developed, permanent form of the ruling group and as the agent of an advanced rationalization of political society. Max Weber did not develop a dynamic, critical theory of the state, but he avoided the mystical trap into which Durkheim fell. Above all, he rediscovered an observation of Proudhon, who drew a parallel between the relation of the state to social life and the relation of religion (or the church) to the moral life. He showed, in fact, the connexion between the development of the state structure and that of ecclesiastical structures, which con- stitute nothing less than a hierocratic power. Weber's analyses foreshadow, in this respect, recent interpretations of the state, including that of the anthropologist Leslie White, who uses the notion of *state/church* and sees, beneath both aspects, the same mechanism of integration and regulation in civil societies.*

2. The Uncertainties of Political Anthropology

These philosophical and sociological guide-lines help us to situate the attempts of political anthropologists to characterize the traditional state and to determine the conditions of its emergence. However, these attempts meet with an as yet un- surmounted difficulty; it is expressed first at the level of the clear distinction between political organization and the state and secondly at the typological level, in so far as State society must be distinguished from related social forms, especially those based on the chiefdom. The definitions proposed are usually too wide and, consequently, non-specific. According to Lowie (1948, p. 317), 'the state embraces the inhabitants of a definite area who acknowledge the legitimacy of force when applied by the individuals whom they accept as rulers or governors'. The territorial framework, the separation of the governed from the governors and the legitimate use of coercion would appear, then, to be the characteristics of the 'primitive' state. In fact, they are necessary, but not adequate, for they also apply to political societies that are regarded as being without a state apparatus. The same uncertainty is to be found in the case of definitions that limit the state to 'the maintenance of public order within fixed territorial limits'. On the other hand, a new

*For Max Weber's political sociology, cf. Weber (1958).

characteristic appears when it is suggested that the state is revealed, in its simplest form, as soon as *a* kinship group acquires the permanent power to direct the collectivity and to impose its will. In this case, the differentiation of a specialized group, extricating itself from the relations established by kinship, possessing a monopoly of power and the privileges that go with power, is presented as the first relevant characteristic. The importance of the territorial criterion and the function of maintaining social order result, in a sense, from this.

The American anthropologist Leslie White wished to define the traditional state by its forms and functions. From the functional point of view, he saw it as assuming responsibility for preserving 'the integrity of the socio-cultural system of which it is a part' – against threats both from within and from without, which implies the ability to mobilize human and material resources and to use an organized force. This role as preserver of 'the system as everything' conceals a more particular function: the maintenance of the relations of subordination and exploitation. The state organization must, in fact, be linked to the 'deep, fundamental cleavage', which lies within *all* forms of civil society, between a dominant, ruling class (kings, nobles, priests and warriors) and a subordinate class (free workers and peasants, serfs, slaves) that produces all the goods required by society. The ancient state already appears as the product of this inequality, which it continues to maintain by protecting the economic system it has built up, by preserving the 'class' structure that it expresses and by striving to contain the forces that seek to destroy it. Like the Marxist theory, which, together with functionalism, inspired it, this interpretation characterizes the state by identifying it with 'the politically organized ruling class'. The specificity of the traditional state must be looked for, in one way, in the overlapping of the political and the religious, which Spencer had already drawn attention to and which White emphasizes when he affirms that the state and the church are only two *aspects* of the political mechanism (1959).

Nadel, who was one of the finest creators of political anthropology, tried to classify the basic notions. He defined political organization by two major characteristics:

1. its capacity of total inclusion: it embraces all the institutions concerned with the direction and preservation of society as a whole;
2. its monopoly of the legitimate use of force and the ultimate sanctions – those against which there is no appeal.

The state is characterized, then, as *a* specific form of political organization. In his great work, *A Black Byzantium* (1942), Nadel posits essentially three criteria of distinction:

1. territorial sovereignty: the state is a political unit based on this sovereignty, it has an inter-tribal or inter-racial base and the membership it confers depends on residence or birth in a determined territory;
2. an apparatus of centralized government that ensures the protection of the law and the maintenance of order, to the exclusion of all independent action;
3. a specialized and privileged ruling group or a class separated by its formation, status and organization from the population as a whole – this group or class monopolizes, as a body, the machinery of political decision.

Nadel sees the state as a particular form of political organization, realized in a certain number of historical and modern cases, of which it is extremely difficult to construct a type; in fact, there are 'transitional forms' that do not possess all the characteristics mentioned above. By carrying Nadel's analysis to its logical conclusion, one might conclude that the traditional state exists more often in a doubtful form than in a fully constituted one.

A more advanced inventory of the definitions borrowed from political anthropology seems to be of little use, for they reflect the difficulties already met with by sociological theories of the state, and reveal less critical rigour than some of these theories. It would be helpful to examine and evaluate the most frequently used criteria.

a. The territorial link

Following Maine and Morgan, Lowie characterizes the primitive state by the role played by the territorial principle, adding, however, that far from being incompatible with the kinship principle, it is distinctive only by the predominance of the local ties that it conditions:

'The basic problem of the state is thus not that of explaining the somersault by which ancient peoples achieved the step from a government by personal relations to one by territorial contiguity only. The question is rather to show what processes strengthened the local tie which must be recognized as not less ancient than the rival principle' (1927, p. 73).

Later, Lowie adds implicitly a criterion of *scale* or *size*, when he affirms that the foundation of the state implies the ability to conceive of a 'unit' that extends beyond the limits of immediate kinship and spatial contiguity. There are therefore two elements: the unit realized within a territorial framework and the extension of the political society subjected to the state apparatus.

Similarly, White sets out to discover how 'localized kinship groups become territorial units within a political system'. This transformation is linked, says White, to changes in the size of clans and tribes: when such changes occur, kinship ties are weakened and the organization of kinship tends to collapse beneath its own weight. The territorial factor then appears predominant: 'By the time a special mechanism of coordination, integration and administration has been developed and kinship has been supplanted by property as the basis of social organization, it is the territorial unit, rather than kinship group, that becomes significant as a principle of political organization'

(1959, p. 310). This interpretation is illustrated by examples of uncontested states. The *ayllu* of the Inca Empire appear originally to have been exogamous matrilineal groups that had become units of standardized size attached to a definite territory, then associated within 'tribes' which, grouped in fours, formed 'provinces', which, in turn, formed the four sections of the Empire, each having an *apo* (viceroy) at its head. Among the Aztecs, the *culpulli* were originally exogamous patrilineal clans; subsequently, at the time of the Spanish conquest, they were localized in distinct districts, each having its own cult, its own council and its own special functionaries; and these districts, which were twenty in number, were divided between the four sections that made up the government frameworks.* By showing that the kinship organization *can* be transformed into a differentiated political organization with a territorial base, the work of anthropologists has revealed three characteristics of this process: the number of men as the determinant of the effacement of kinship, the organization of space to political ends and the appearance of the property tie entering into competition with certain of the ancient personal relations.

The relations between the three terms – kinship, territory and the political – cannot be reduced to a single model. At a very early date, ancient China and Japan developed complex structures that were both territorial and political; so much so that the cadastral survey not only made it possible to draw up an inventory of resources, but became an instrument for influencing the division of wealth and power. In the Tonga archipelago, in Polynesia, a centralized political organization was able to establish itself, extend its territory to the point of becoming a maritime empire and survive. The *Tui Tonga*, the hierarchs, built up a state that is a unique phenomenon in the Pacific area. Relations based on kinship and the localized patrilineal group continue to operate, however, but the first contains within itself distinctions of rank and hierarchy and the second is dominated by a system of territorial powers established in the provinces. These authorities

*A brief description is to be found in G. P. Murdock (1934).

are legitimized by the possession of territorial rights, conceded by the sovereign to his representatives, which reduces the occupants to a mere right of use and imposes on them an 'annual homage' consisting of a heavy tribute in kind (cf. Gifford, 1929). In Black Africa, the situation is highly diversified. The political structures are usually distinct from the territorial structures: the master of the land, or his equivalent, is next in position to the chief; the clan authorities coexist (somewhat uneasily) with the authorities that emanate from the state power; land ownership is usually differentiated from sovereignty.

An example from Africa may provide a more detailed picture of the system of relations established with the territory and with the land. The kingdom of Buganda (in Uganda), which is now [or rather was, until very recently] a modernist autocracy, was established in the eighteenth and nineteenth centuries and undoubtedly possesses a complex state structure. A Ganda proverb suggests that power over men (the political relation) is quite different from power over land (the land tie): 'The chief does not command the land, but men.' In fact, the separation is neither so clear nor so simple as a division of rights, even if one ignores the profound changes brought about, since 1900, by a colonization that set out to create a landed aristocracy. On the one hand, the patri-clans and patrilineages are tied to the land on which the clan authorities (the *bataka*) reside and the tombs of the revered ancestors are situated. These relations are governed by the inheritance and continuity created by the descent system, but the clans do not form territorial units; membership of a clan does not necessarily determine residence and local communities are heterogeneous. On the other hand, the political hierarchy that emanates from the sovereign consists of different levels determined either by competence or by territorial influence: provinces, districts, village groups. The decree of the king and the relations of personal dependence ensure the organization of the state, which must be defined, in a certain way, as the network formed by the 'king's men': chiefs called *bakungu* (some of which are hereditary posts) and functionaries called *batongole*, who are dependents of the king and deal above all with village affairs. Both may be given 'fiefs' that go with their posts – which means that they are of a precarious nature – and the king himself possesses his own private patrimony in the form of 'estates' scattered throughout the various provinces. Power, then, is deeply rooted in the land in every region of the kingdom. On the other hand, certain clan chiefs, who have remained the guardians of the lands proper to their clans, have acquired functions of authority, or prestige, within the political and administrative organization, while the others are confined to domestic affairs or are eliminated altogether.

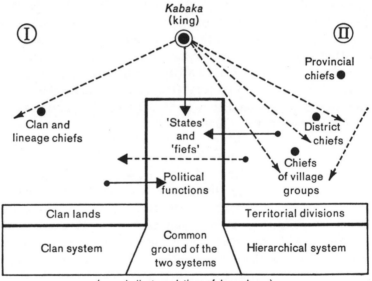

(---→ indicates relations of dependence)

This example shows the effacement of the political functions assumed by the descent groups (correlative to the reinforcement of the state), the place accorded to the territorial structure, which is the basis of the politico-administrative apparatus, the constitution of land rights outside clan lands, the overlapping of a segmentary system, based on kinship, which continues to carry land rights, and a centralized hierarchical system, based on the administrative divisions of the territory and on the relations of personal dependence. A simplified diagram (see opposite page) might make these various aspects clearer.

This diagram might lead one to give prime importance to the territorial factor in the constitution of the traditional state, in so far as section II clearly dominates section I. Nevertheless, the existence of a large area of common ground between the two sections shows that the clan system (segmentary) and the state system (centralized) do overlap and are, to a certain extent, concurrent.

b. The segmentary and the centralized

The state is regarded as logically a centralizing factor and the capital – the spatial centre of power – concretizes this supremacy over local or private powers. Such, as least, is the most commonly recognized historical process. However, in its ancient form, because of technical and economic conditions and the survival of social relations that were hardly compatible with its own power, the state finds it difficult to carry this logic to its conclusion. Already Ibn Khaldoûn, in his *Mouqaddima*, the introduction to his *Universal History*, had observed that every dynasty can govern only a limited area and loses its power in its outlying regions; 'A dynasty is much more powerful at its centre than in its outlying regions. When it has extended its authority to its utmost limits, it grows weak' (Ibn Khaldoûn, 1965). Arab sociology is well aware, then, of the problems involved in the arrangement of space to political ends. If the instruments at the disposal of the centralized power are to remain effective, they are bound to rest heavily on technical advance *and* the material and intellectual communications media. A number of African empires – from the empires of western Sudan to the Kongo and the Lunda empire – and kingdoms have disintegrated because they covered too vast an area.

The use of itinerant (or multiple) capitals is an attempt to over-come these difficulties; if the central power is unable to estab-lish its domination equally, it distributes it by moving its seat. The kings of Buganda have used this procedure and, at the same time, increased the number of their direct representatives in the provinces.

These conditions, within which power must be exercised, necessarily limit centralization and affect the organization and development of the 'traditional' state. The sovereign associates himself with the local holders of power, either by linking them in some way to his court, or by creating local functions that counterbalance or even supplant them. Thus the *kabaka* (kings) of Buganda have given responsibilities to certain clan chiefs, formed lineages that are subject to their control and set up in the provinces posts of authority that create competition and equi-librium favourable to their interests. The difficulties of centrali-zation frequently lead to another result. The relative weakness of the central power allows the maintenance in various parts of the territory of powers that are similar, but *subordinate*, to its own. In this case, the provinces reproduce, in a way, the structures of a state that lacks the means of achieving, in a material sense, its own unity. Thus the Lunda sovereigns of Central Africa have a governor, the *sanama*, to represent them in the southern regions of the empire; this official bases his politico-military organiza-tion on that of the central region. This characteristic is revealed with great clarity in the ancient Kongo kingdom. The king, the provincial chiefs and those of the vassal territories are placed, each at his respective level, in an identical situation and the political arrangement has a repetitive air: the chiefs resemble the sovereign, the small capitals resemble San Salvador, where the king resides (Balandier, 1956). The third consequence is that in so far as the territorial structure of the state remains segmentary, that is, made up of homologous, though hier-archized, elements, there is a high risk of rupture and secession. When the state is weakened, it does not bring the whole of society crashing down to ruin; it gradually contracts and the area it controls is finally limited to the region of which the declining capital is the centre. This process is apparent in certain African traditional states, including Kongo.

The problem of the ability of the 'centre' to control its political territory as a whole is also to be found in traditional societies subject to an absolute power that has an efficient government apparatus at its disposal. K. Wittfogel shows this quite clearly in his controversial book, *Oriental Despotism* (1964). Total despotic power, while quick to suppress separatist movements, finds its most constricting limitations in its relation to space, despite the bureaucratic and material means at its disposal. After linking this form of political organization with 'hydraulic civilization' – based on the regulation of water – Wittfogel observes that it has failed to distribute its own institutions with equal success. Within this system even the *largest* political units are affected by discontinuity and a slackening of cohesion. A historical accident reveals and exploits this weakness, as in the case of northern China, which, on several occasions, invaded 'nomadic tribes', then divided itself into several provinces, each retaining its own 'traditional agro-despotic power structures'. In this case, too, the strain on the state brought with it territorial segmentation and a reduction in its geographical extent, but it did not radically alter the nature of its power. An American example is very significant: that of the Inca empire, which has often been the subject of false interpretations. This, again, was a 'hydraulic' society with a despotic political power. The empire had been built up by successive conquests and had preserved the appearance of a disparate world; it was composed of states, confederations, tribes and rural communities that had preserved their individuality; it superimposed on these diversified units standardized administrative divisions and a rigid organization of the political area that has been called a bureaucratic fiction; its purpose was rather the running of an economy functioning in the interests of the Inca caste than the administration of men, which was very largely conceded to local powers. A. Métraux has emphasized this aspect: 'In fact, the Inca empire combined the most absolute despotism with tolerance towards the social and political order of the subject populations.' Métraux has drawn attention to the survival of regional customs and structures, and to the limits that confronted Inca despotism, for although the state was not entirely centralized, it at least wished to be (1961, pp. 85 ff.). The political area was never homogeneous, despite appearances to the contrary, and the central power compromised with provincial separatisms, despite its absolutism.

The debate of the segmentary and the centralized is not understood by reference only to the territory that the traditional state holds under its jurisdiction. It is situated within the state organization itself, whose unitary tendency it contradicts, and often takes the form of a precarious co-existence between the state structures and the clan or lineage structures. They are, in fact, in a relation of relative incompatibility, and, in certain circumstances, of opposition. The contrast between them can easily be accentuated: segmentary arrangement/hierarchical arrangement, polycentric power/centralized power, egalitarian values/aristocratic values, etc. Certain political anthropologists have emphasized this contrast. Fallers uses as the principal hypothesis of his study of the Soga of Uganda the existence of a 'structural antagonism' between the hierarchical state and the lineage organization. D. Apter finds a 'fundamental cleavage' between the two authority systems and the two series of values that they imply. But the division is never a very rigorous one: while dominating the old clan order, the state order ensures its partial integration; while imposing his domination, the sovereign may present himself as situated at the meeting-point of both, *as king and head of the clans* – which is the case in Buganda.

In societies in which the state has had difficulty in being established, and sometimes is the result of external action (in Tahiti and Hawaii, for example), the confrontation of the two systems and their precarious adjustment appears in all clarity. Polynesia is a valuable illustration in this respect. At Tonga, which has known 'a thousand years of absolute monarchy and divine right' (Guiart, 1963, p. 661), and thus remains an exception among Polynesian societies, the insular dispersion has nevertheless favoured the maintenance of the lineage groups on which the political organization is based, for it is within these groups that the Tongan aristocratic system finds its basis, and it is in relation to them that the relations between the islands are established and the political strategies conceived. In Samoa, the territorial division (into districts) coexists with the division along clan lines and serves as a basis for chiefdoms controlled by an assembly (*fono*). A 'supreme chief', combining in his person titles appertaining to several districts, embodies the political unity of the islands as a whole. The equilibrium, adjusting his power to the local and clan powers, seems so vulnerable that the relevant characteristic of the political organization is the division of the country into two 'parts' – one dominant, powerful one (*malo*), the other (*vaivai*) possessing a conditional power, subject to the decisions of the first. The position of power allows one group or district to exploit the others to the point at which a conflict brings about a change of role. The history of Samoa, up to the twentieth century, consists of these power struggles rather than the gradual development of an embryonic state. In Tahiti, the territorial units seem to correspond with the various zones of influence of the clans. Regional powers succeeded in becoming established and one clan – *Teva* – gained a position of dominance, but the power relations, expressed in revocable alliances, have prevented the establishment of a lasting supremacy. Within the *Teva* group itself, two 'branches' are in a relation of rivalry and dispute control of the clan. The system is characterized by relative instability, and it was only about 1815 – and for mainly external reasons – that Pomaré II, having 'practically exterminated the class of chiefs', had to be regarded as the king of Tahiti. In Williamson's terms, the emergent 'despotic' power had to destroy the 'tribal system' or succumb; with the support of the British (missionaries and others), he temporarily succeeded (1924, vol. 1).

The permanence of the segmentary aspects within the traditional state led Southall to contrast the fully developed, *unitary* state and the *segmentary* state, and to state that the first of these political forms is rarely achieved: 'In many parts of the world, and at most times, the degree of political specialization attained has been of the segmentary rather than the unitary type' (1956, p. 254). The power structure, which is the main distinctive criterion, is said to be 'pyramidal' in the first case. Similar powers are repeated at each level; the constitutive units possess a relative autonomy, a territory that is not merely an administrative division and an administrative apparatus; their respective relations remain similar to those that link the segments to each other within a clan society; lastly, the whole system often appears more centralized at the ritual level than at the level of political action. In the second case, the structure is said to be *hierarchical*, in the sense that the powers are clearly differentiated, according to the level at which they are situated, and that the supreme power exercises unquestioned domination.

Southall lists six characteristics of the segmentary state:

1. territorial sovereignity is recognized, but limited – its authority declines as one moves from the centre to the outlying regions;

2. the centralized government coexists with centres of power over which it exercises only relative control;

3. the centre possesses a specialized administration that is to be found, on a smaller scale, in the various zones;

4. the central authority does not possess an absolute monopoly of the legitimate use of force;

5. the levels of subordination are distinct, but their relations remain of a pyramidal character: for each of them, authority conforms to the same model;

6. the subordinate authorities are able to change allegiance the more they are situated towards the periphery (1956, chapter 9).

This important theoretical contribution deserves a critical examination. First of all, it ignores the following fact: in order that the hierarchical power structure should clearly predominate, the *preponderant* social relations must themselves be of a hierarchical type, that is to say, the orders (or estates), castes and proto-classes must predominate over the relations of a repetitive type that result from descent and alliance. Moreover, it establishes too radical a break between hierarchical and pyramidal relations, which in fact coexist in traditional states and in several modern states – in the case of the former, this has been shown in examples provided by political anthropology. Lastly, the role of competition and conflict within political action itself means that political action retains a segmentary aspect.

The ruling group is no more perfectly unitary than is the state. Its constitutive elements compete for power, prestige and wealth; and this competition requires strategies that exploit, at least provisionally, the segmentary divisions of society as a whole. The play of coalitions may contradict the formation of the state (the case of Polynesia), or cause wars of succession that inaugurate a period during which there is a power vacuum (the case of the traditional states of Africa). The same can be said of the competition for posts that require support from members of the political élite, and personal power (a 'party') consisting of relations, allies and dependents.* Personal positions in the ruling hierarchy are therefore reinforced by the system of 'segmentary' relations.

c. The rationality of the traditional state

For the theoretical sociologists who follow Weber, the state is the result of the slow rationalization of the existing political structures, expressed in a desire for unity, a competent administration dealing with explicit regulations and a tendency to

*Cf. the contribution by P. C. Lloyd to the A.S.A. symposium, *Political Systems and Distribution of Power*, London, 1965.

organize the *whole* of the collective life. In a great many traditional states, rationality in this sense rarely occurs: unity and rationalization remain incomplete and vulnerable, the separatist rights remain, the administration is based on situations of status and on relations of personal dependence rather than on competence, the state power hardly intervenes (and to an unequal degree, depending on distance from the centre) in local affairs. It is only in the type of 'oriental despotism' developed by Wittfogel that rationality is accentuated – or exacerbated. The characteristics regarded as specific are revealing: the state holds total power and the ruling class is identified with the state *apparatus*; it is the master of the essential means of production and plays an enormous role in the economy; it establishes control of the bureaucracy and creates, in the society it dominates, a *bureaucratic* land ownership, a *bureaucratic* capitalism and a *bureaucratic* rural aristocracy. This form of state, which enables it to become stronger than society, is explained by a whole range of conditions and means: by restriction of private property and supreme control over large-scale technological enterprises; by the efficient organization of communications and the possession of a monopoly of military action, by the existence of a system of census and records, which is necessary to the functioning of a fiscal system that provides the government with a permanent revenue; by the subjection of the dominant religion, which gives the regime a hierocratic or theocratic character (Wittfogel, 1957, Introduction, chapters 2, 3).

This ideal type, in Weber's sense, is not to be found in all the 'hydraulic societies' listed by Wittfogel, as the analysis of the obstacles to and limitation on centralization has shown. It is also of limited use in the case of the societies that gave rise to its formulation. In ancient China, despite 'despotism' and the expansion of the bureaucratic system, the political structure remained largely segmentary; under the official hierarchy broadly autonomous units – villages, clans, guilds – were maintained, and the state power acted as arbitrator when their interests came into conflict. Weber compares the 'primitive administrative structure' of China with that of the African kingdoms; he emphasizes the loss of authority from the centre to the periphery, the vigour of the hereditary factor, the role of the clan structure within the political system and the varying function of the theocratic and charismatic elements. The rationality inherent in the institutions of the despotic traditional state is confined within limits that contradict its attainment. Yet it is led to the point at which the ruling group acquires and preserves *its own optimum of rationality* – or approaches this state, which is seen in terms of the possession of wealth, symbols and prestige.

An example would give greater point to this analysis. Because of the size of the kingdom, its survival until a quite recent date and the quality of the ethnographical information about it, monarchical Rwanda would seem to be a particularly happy one. A dominant minority of foreign origin, the *Tutsi* group, imposed its rule over a large, native, peasant majority (over 82 per cent), the *Hutu*. It gradually built up the state, extended the territory and set up the machinery necessary for its political and economic control: the network of relations of personal dependence, the politico-administrative hierarchy and the army. It ensured security and encouraged the capitalization of manpower to such a degree that the population density exceeded 100 inhabitants per square kilometre in its final decades. Lastly, it built up a unitary system of which the sovereign, the absolute master of men and the country, was the guardian and developed a rational culture. However, the rationality proper to the Rwanda state met with a number of obstacles. The regions were less and less subject to state control the farther away they were from the centre, the clan and lineage structures increased in vigour as this control was relaxed; as a result, the balance between the various powers altered in the same conditions. The state was unable to establish its authority evenly, and the 'regional' variants reveal the limitations on the spread of the administrative system. These resistances are explained not only by inadequate techniques (those concerning the means of arranging the territory and ensuring communications and those inherent in a rudimentary bureaucracy), they were also a resistance to the domination of the Tutsi aristocracy. The rationality of the Rwandese system was not so much that of a state, organizing society as a whole, as that of a 'class', organizing the exploitation of a peasant majority concerned with production and subject to innumerable levies. The socio-political mechanism functioned with this purpose in mind. If one attempts to represent graphically the arrangement of the fundamental social relations – which all have economic implications – one realizes that they are directed towards the sovereign (*mwami*), the agents of the political-administrative hierarchy and the aristocracy.

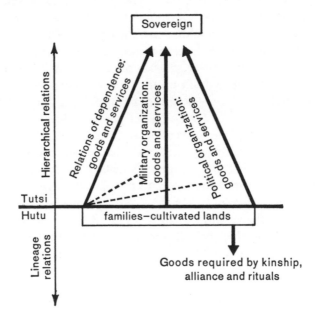

This rationality, operating to the advantage of the dominant ruling minority, is so incontestable that the political organization could be interpreted as 'an exchange system'. The king, the chiefs and the elders had to possess considerable wealth in order to be able to make gifts and thus express their superiority.* The Tutsi and Hutu were seen, and in a sense saw each other, as essentially foreign groups that the play of *unequal* exchange had brought together. A highly constructed ideology expressed this fundamental inequality; it saw Tutsi domination as grounded both in nature and in history, because it resulted from a divine decree. J. Vansina pointed out that, for the court historiographers, 'the Rwanda past was the history of the practically uninterrupted progress of a chosen people, the Tutsis, whose royal dynasty was descended from the heavens'. While the state is still imperfectly constituted, its ambiguity is apparent: it is the instrument used by a minority group to ensure its domination, yet it is presented as the emanation of a transcendent rationality acting to the advantage of society as a whole. This view contradicts, however, the interpretations of several anthropologists, including Malinowski, who have concerned themselves with political problems.

d. The characteristics of the traditional state

Malinowski believes that 'the primitive state is not tyrannical to its own subjects' (1947, p. 266). He finds the explanation for this non-oppressive characteristic in the fact that the fundamental relations remain those created by kinship, clan membership, the system of age-groups, etc., by which 'everybody is related, really or fictitiously, to everybody else' (Malinowski, 1947, p. 253). The personalization of social and political relations would therefore provide a distinction between the primitive state and the bureaucratic state, and would result in the elimination (or reduction) of the gap between the state power and the society subjected to its jurisdiction. This view is contradicted by the facts – though it quite rightly emphasizes the personal aspect of authority. It is partially verified only in so far as the state is

*Cf. the study by A. Troubworst (1961) of the neighbouring (and similar) kingdom of Burundi.

still at an embryonic stage and has not yet appropriated the political power of the society. But this idyllic vision has led some specialists to see the state as 'a great family' comprising a whole people.

Basing his analysis on the results of African research, Gluckman has emphasized characteristics proper to African state societies and regarded them as having wider application. After mentioning the limitations of technology, the low differentiation of the economy in a number of cases and the role still played by 'mechanical solidarity', he goes on to demonstrate the intrinsic *instability* of these states. They are threatened with segmentation more by the fragility of their territorial base than by the type of power of which they are the instrument. Their physical vulnerability, one might say, contrasts with the capacity for resistance shown by the political organization that they imply. What is the explanation for this apparent contradiction? Gluckman speaks of the absence of cleavages and conflicts between the economic interests of the governors and governed: the 'class' conflict does not yet operate and the system of power and authority is not fundamentally questioned. Conflict is reduced to that inherent in the system, that is, to the struggle for power and position. Gluckman completes his theory by saying that 'African states contained within themselves a process of constant rebellion, but not revolution' (1963, p. 9). It is not their structures that are in question, but only the holders of power and authority. Rebellion then leads to secessions and changes in the holders of office, and may even be institutionalized as a factor in the strengthening of the political organization, within the framework of a periodical ritual (cf. in particular Gluckman, 1955, 1963). The internal dynamisms of the traditional state are thus recognized as a form of instability affecting the extension of the political territory, rivalries for power and rebellions lacking in revolutionary effectiveness; while the forces of change depend more on external conditions than on contestation acting within the system. This interpretation is only partly true, for it underestimates the constraint exercised by the state – a constraint which, for Murdock, on the contrary, was later to suggest a type of 'African despotism', much as it avoided opposition between unequal social groups, between governors and governed. The study of *social movements* in the societies that come within the scope of anthropology must be undertaken if the false image of the nature of the traditional state societies is to be corrected. This development is in fact taking place. Thus, in a recent theoretical essay, Lloyd emphasizes the inevitable nature of conflict and the necessary recourse to coercion that characterizes *any* state, and defines the areas in which conflict is expressed: within the 'political elite', between the sub-groups that make up that elite, within society as a whole and between the privileged minority and the 'masses' subjected to the domination of this minority. Fried takes up the systematic study of the correlations between social stratification and state forms and concludes that all state power is the instrument of inequality.

It is difficult to see how it could be otherwise. The traditional state cannot be defined by a sociological type (or model) that would oppose it *radically* to the modern state. In so far as it is a state, it conforms first of all to common characteristics. As a differentiated, specialized and permanent organ of political and administrative action, it requires *an* apparatus of government capable of ensuring security internally and at its frontiers. It is applied to a territory and organizes the political area in such a way that this arrangement corresponds to the hierarchy of power and authority, and ensures the execution of basic decisions in the whole country under its jurisdiction. As a means of domination, held by a minority with the monopoly of political decision-making, it is situated above the society whose common interests it must none the less defend. As a result, the traditional state organization is an essentially dynamic system, involving the permanent use of strategies that maintain its supremacy and that of the group that controls it. New anthropological research demands that these aspects should not be neglected (or ignored): the traditional state allows a minority to exercise lasting domination; the struggles for power within that minority – and politics in these societies is often little more than this – do more to strengthen rather than to weaken the domination exercised. During these struggles the political class 'hardens' and the power it holds as a group moves towards its maximum point. These characteristics are most strongly emphasized in the type known as 'oriental despotism'.

The traditional state also possesses distinctive characteristics. Some of these have already been discussed. The traditional state is bound to exercise a large degree of empiricism; it is created out of pre-existing political units that it cannot abolish and on which its own structures are based; it manages only inadequately to impose the supremacy of the political centre and preserves a diffused quality that distinguishes it from the modern centralized state; it is constantly threatened with territorial segmentation. Moreover, this form of political organization usually corresponds to the *patrimonialism* defined by Weber. The sovereign holds power by virtue of personal qualities (and not external and formal criteria) and by means of a mandate from heaven, the gods or the royal ancestors that allows him to act in the name of a tradition regarded as inviolable and to demand a submission the refusal of which is tantamount to sacrilege. Power and authority are so strongly personalized that it is difficult to distinguish between the public interest, proper to the function, and the private interest of the office holder. The governmental and administrative apparatus uses dignitaries and notables, whose loyalty is secured by relations of personal dependence, rather than officials.

Political strategies seem to be specific to this type of power: they involve relations of kinship and alliance, relations between patron and client, the various procedures for increasing the number of dependents and the ritual means that give the political power its sacred base. In the second place, political antagonisms may be expressed by setting the lineal order against the hierarchical order established by the state, or by seeing them in terms of a religious or magical confrontation. Lastly, the relation with the sacred always remains apparent, for it is by referring to it that the traditional state defines its legitimacy, develops its most revered symbols and expresses part of its characteristic ideology. In a way, its theoretical rationality is expressed in the dominant religion, just as its practical rationality is expressed in the group (or proto-class) that possesses the monopoly of power.

3. Hypotheses on the Origin of the State

Anthropology has long entertained the ambition of elucidating the origins of the earliest primitive institutions, and it has never completely abandoned that ambition. The problem of the origin of the state is one of those which, because of the theoretical elaborations they periodically give rise to, have been present intermittently throughout the history of the discipline. It was considered at length by the founders and continues to dominate certain recent work. However, a summary of the results of these studies seems rather disappointing, though they do help us to understand the various characteristics of the primitive state, and to reveal the ambiguities that affect the definition of state power. The scientific interest of these theoretical enterprises is nil as soon as one accepts – as W. Koppers suggests – that the state dates back to the earliest stages in human history. It becomes more apparent in the more numerous interpretations that link the formative process of state power to the fact of *conquest*, seen as the creator of differentiation, inequality and domination. In *Der Staat* (1907), F. Oppenheimer defines all known states by the fact of the domination of one class over another with a view to economic exploitation. He links the formation of the 'class system', and the resulting establishment of a state power, to *external* intervention: the subjugation of an indigenous group by a foreign and conquering group. This point of view is accepted, with certain nuances and variations, by several anthropologists, some of whom show, none the less, genuine theoretical rigour. Linton, for example, sees two basic ways of constructing states: voluntary association and domination imposed by virtue of superior force. The second seems to him to be the most frequent: 'States may come into being either through the federation of two or more tribes or through the subjugation of weak groups by stronger ones, with the loss of their autonomy ... Conquest states are much more numerous than confederacies' (1936, pp. 240–43). In *An Introduction to Anthropology*, published in 1953, R. Beals and H. Hoijer still consider, and with fewer reservations, that the exclusive right to use force and coercion legitimately – the right by which the governmental power is defined – appears only with the conquest state. Similarly, Nadel, among the theoretical considerations that accompany his study of the political system of the Nupe (Nigeria), regards conquest as one of the factors that seem to be necessary to the formation of state power (1942, pp. 69–70).

This mode of interpretation is also associated with a long line of specialists working outside the field of anthropology. These include Oppenheimer, mentioned above, L. Gumplowicz (*Grundriss der Soziologie*, 1905) and Weber, who, defining the political by the fact of domination, sees external conquest as constituting this relation. In a more recent work, A. Rüstow still adheres to the theory of the exogenous development of complex social stratifications and of a political power that he calls *feudal* (1950–52). Despite the persistence of this 'explanation' – which H. E. Barnes has raised to the dignity of a 'sociologically distinctive theory of the origin of the state' – its limitations were soon exposed by criticism. On the basis of material concerning the North American Indians, W. MacLeod pointed out the essentially endogenous development of certain social hierarchies and of the political power that they condition (1924, pp. 12, 39). But, of the early anthropologists, it was Lowie who questioned this theory most forcefully. He remarked that 'internal conditions may suffice to create hereditary or approximately hereditary classes' and, through these, the primitive state, and observes that the two main factors – unequal differentiation and conquest – 'are not necessarily incompatible' (1927, p. 42). However, by wishing to show the internal characteristics favourable to the formation of state power, he takes up an extreme position and sees the presence of this power in the *potential* states of a large number of human societies. Elsewhere he says: 'In a very ancient period and in a very primitive environment, it was not necessary to break the links of kinship in order to found a political state. In fact, side by side with the family and the clan, there existed for countless centuries associations such as masculine "clubs", age groups or secret organizations, independent of kinship, moving so to speak in a quite different sphere from that of the kinship group and capable of taking on quite easily a political character, if they did not do so at their appearance.' In short, Lowie posits essentially two internal conditions favourable to the establishment of the primitive state: the existence of social relations outside kinship, some of which involve the principle of 'local contiguity', and the existence of groups called 'associations' that create inequality on the basis of sex, age or initiation. But the difficulty is in no way diminished: these characteristics are general ones and all the societies that possess them have very diverse forms of political organization. Lowie is obliged therefore to make use of factors that are less widespread and which bring about the process of the centralization of political power. Some of these are of an internal kind: the importance of military associations, even if it is only of a seasonal character as among the Cheyenne Indians; the predominance of hierarchies established according to rank, as in Polynesian societies; the presence of strongly sacralized individuals who found an autocracy by surrounding their activities with the 'halo of the supernatural'. The others are of an external kind: the intervention of foreigners, who settle and and who provide the local chiefs with additional power, as in Fiji; conquest, which causes an extension of the political unit and creates domination, as of several African kingdoms and empires. Lowie, then, sees several ways that lead to centralized power, but ignores *the economic conditions* that create the social relations, which, in turn, make that power necessary. Moreover, his excessively wide definition of the state leads him to recognize an embryonic state power as soon as 'the potential and permanent use of physical constraint' has been 'sanctioned by the community'. This over-exclusive interpretation does not help to determine with sufficient rigour the constitutive processes of the most highly developed traditional states (Lowie, 1927; 1948, chapter 14).

Thanks to more recent anthropological research, the relative role of conquest in the totality of these processes has been revalued. Fried suggests that a clear distinction should be drawn between *primary* states and *secondary* or derived states. The first are those that have been formed, by means of internal or regional development, without the stimulus of other pre-existing state forms. There are fewer of these: the states of the Nile valley and of Mesopotamia – the centres of the earliest state societies – and those of China, Peru and Mexico. The second result from a 'response' imposed by the presence of a neighbouring state, a power centre that eventually modifies the equilibrium established over a wide area. A number of state societies in Asia, Europe and Africa have been built up by this method – though in different ways. Examining the African kingdoms and empires, H. Lewis identifies some of the processes that contributed, in a secondary way, to their formation:

1. rapid or insidious conquest operating to the detriment of weakened political units (kingdoms of the interlacustrian region in East Africa);

2. war that brings about, through victory and defeat, a new political configuration (Galla, in Ethiopia);

3. secession resulting from the ambition of the local agents of the central power (Mossi) or from a revolt against tribute (Dahomey);

4. voluntary submission to a foreign power regarded as being efficient (Shambala, in Tanzania) (Lewis, 1966).

With its distinction between the two ways in which states are formed, this approach is similar to the one Wittfogel applied to 'conquest society', using a distinction between *primary* conquest, which creates an advanced social stratification, and *secondary* conquest, which leads to a greater differentiation of the stratified societies. Indirectly both pose the problem of endogenous development, without which the effects considered here would be unable to take place in already stratified societies possessing a strong political power. Both have the same implications: they show the importance and complexity of external influences and the limitations of theories based on the fact of conquest alone. The political effects of external factors, of externally orientated relations, become even more obvious when one remembers that all power obeys a double necessity, one of an internal and another of an external order. A variant of what might be called the relational interpretations of the origin of primitive states is offered by A. Southall. He sees ethnic and cultural *heterogeneity*, within the same region, as being a condition favourable to the realization of this process. The interaction of diversified ethnic groups, with contrasting social structures, predisposes them to assume a domination/subordination structure on the basis of which a state power can be built up. According to Southall, two circumstances favour this development. One of the groups *already* possesses an effective *large-scale* political organization: it has at its disposal the means of politically controlling a larger area and eventually imposes its supremacy on the micro-societies with which it is in relation. One of the groups contains *charismatic* leaders, who become the chiefs solicited by the neighbouring societies or the 'models' according to which they organize the internal power by subordinating it. The establishment of a structure of domination is made possible in the one case by the ability to govern a large political area and in the second by the quality of the leader. At this stage an embryonic state is in being.

All these theories come up against a difficulty that they all attempt to overcome with the same weapons: failing to discover within the pre-state societies adequate conditions for the formation of the state, they seek the differential gap that makes possible the establishment of relations of domination outside the societies themselves.

In the implicit or explicit anthropology outlined by Marxism, it is the internal process of transformation that is given pride of place – namely, the change from the primitive community to a society in which the state becomes the principal mechanism of social integration, the principal unifier. In his famous work on *The Origin of the Family, Private Property and the State*, Engels does not ignore the conquest theory. He uses this theory, together with demographic characteristics, to explain the origin of state power among the Teutons, which he sees as a direct result of 'the conquest of vast foreign territories that the regime of the *gens* provided no means of dominating'. But it was in Athens that he saw 'the purest, most classical form', in which the state was born *directly* from the antagonisms already present in the society of the *gentes*. He considers five circumstances to be particularly favourable to the transcending of a mere tribal confederation: the creation of a central administration and a body of national law; the division of the citizens into three 'classes'; the dissolving action of the monetary economy; the appearance of private property; the substitution of the territorial link for the link of consanguinity. At the end of complex and convergent processes, the state sets itself above all the 'class' divisions of society, to the advantage of those who possess the means of exploitation. After comparing the formation of the state in Athens, in Rome and among the Teutons, Engels draws general conclusions that remain of unquestionable theoretical importance and which have inspired a number of political anthropologists – who, very often, have failed to acknowledge their debt. They may be summarized in the three following propositions: the state is born from society; it appears when society is in 'insoluble contradiction with itself' and its function is to reduce the conflict by keeping it within the bounds of order; it is defined as 'a power, sprung from society, but which wishes to place itself above society and to separate itself more and more from society'.

But Engels has not solved all the difficulties, for in the end he retains a unilinear concept of social and political development, by eliminating previous considerations concerning the Asiatic mode of production and oriental despotism, and by ignoring the anthropological data derived from certain primitive states. In fact, he regards the movement of western history as typical of the development of societies and civilizations in general, while recognizing that this movement itself breaks down into various currents when it leads to the formation of state organizations. But the direction given by Engels remains fruitful. It encourages the identification of transitional forms – those that still possess aspects of communal society *and* already possess aspects of a 'class' (or proto-class) society with an established state power. The urgent task now is *the search for different processes by which inequality is established and by which contradictions appear within society* and necessitate the formation of a differentiated organism whose function is to contain them. Depending at present on progress gained in the field of economic anthropology, and in the history of the societies studied by the anthropologists, this enterprise may create, at least for a time, a lack of interest in the endless consideration of the origin of state power.

Chapter Seven

Tradition and Modernity

Before reaching maturity, political anthropology must first undergo the tests to which any anthropological work is now submitted. The old forms of power are declining and changing; primitive governments and traditional states, together with their bureaucracies, are disappearing – or transforming themselves. The political mutation has begun in most of the so-called developing countries and is replacing the readjustments brought about by colonial domination or dependence. In a number of cases – many, though by no means all, from Asia, which has been open for so long to outside influences – this mutation is extending a long political history largely determined by the interplay of *external relations*. In Polynesia – Samoa, Tahiti and Hawaii – 'centralized monarchies' resulted from European activities and ideas (eighteenth century), then disappeared or declined under the law of the colonizers. In Black Africa those political entities possessing an outlet to the western coasts – notably in the region of the Gulf of Guinea and in the Congolese region – were affected by their century-old relations with Europeans; some of them, before undergoing their destructive effects, saw these relations as providing the conditions for their own reinforcement. Thus, in the kingdom of Kongo, which established links with Portugal at the end of the fifteenth century, the representatives of the Portuguese sovereign at the capital suggested an institutional reform, defined by a *regimento*, which took effect from the beginning of the sixteenth century.

The most remarkable political modifications are not only the product of recent influences; but after operating for a long period in a number of traditional societies, they are now changing their nature by being expressed in a more vigorous, more radical way and by being more generalized. For this very reason, political anthropology cannot ignore the dynamisms and historical movement that are transforming the systems of institutions that it is studying, and must create dynamic models that are capable of taking political changes into account and identifying the tendencies for change within the structures and organizations. Its work is not confined to what, a few years ago, we were pleased to call primitive forms of government, for it remains in the presence of a wide diversity of political societies and highly complex forms of traditionalism. It studies a great many experiments – some of them quite new – thus increasing and differentiating the information that enables it to become the comparative science of politics and modes of government.

1. Agents and Aspects of Political Change

The transformation of traditional political systems outside Europe and White America is generally linked to modern colonization or to its attenuated variant, dependence. Apter (1965) regards colonialism as 'a modernizing force', as 'a model by which modernization has been universalized'. The correctness of this statement becomes apparent if one considers the breaks, the effects of destructuralization, the new modes of organization that have resulted from colonial enterprise and constraint. However, this general statement must be replaced by a deeper analysis of the *immediate political consequences* of the colonial situation. In reference to colonized Africa, where these phenomena appear in an exaggerated form, five main features may be distinguished.

a. The denaturation of the traditional political units

With few exceptions, the frontiers created by the accidents of colonization do not coincide with the political frontiers established in the course of African history, or with areas possessing cultural similarities. In this respect, the old kingdom of Kongo is one of the most significant examples, since the territory it had controlled and organized for several centuries was broken up by colonial division and is now divided between the two modern Congo states and Angola, where its former capital is situated. And today historical memories help to maintain a nostalgia for a lost unity.

b. Degradation by depoliticalization

When the traditional political unit was not destroyed, because of its opposition to the establishment of the colonizers (the case of the old kingdom of Dahomey), it was reduced none the less to a conditional existence. Colonization transformed every political problem into a *technical* problem to be dealt with by the administration. It contained every expression of communal life and every action that seemed to limit or threaten its grip, irrespective of the forms of the native political society and the colonial regimes that organized their domination. Within the framework of the colonial situation real political life was expressed partly in a clandestine way or during a period of real transfer of power. The *doubling* of the administratively recognized authorities by the effective, though unseen authorities, which enlightened administrators saw as an obstacle to their action, illustrates the first process. Politically significant reactions also operated in an *indirect* way and appeared where they could find expression, notably in the new religious movements and prophetic and messianic churches that proliferated after 1920, or under cover of an apparently unpolitical traditionalism and neo-traditionalism.

The colonized peoples often used, with great strategic skill, the cultural gap that separated them from the colonizers.

c. The break in traditional systems of limiting power

The relation established between power and public opinion, the mechanisms that ensure the consent of the governed, notably those involving the sacred, are disturbed by the very existence of the colonial administrations. The governors now act only under control and become less responsible to their subjects; the spokesmen of the people – the counterparts of those who intercede with the chiefs among the Ashanti of Ghana – lose their function. The sovereigns now possess a more arbitrary, though more limited power, and the acquiescence of the colonial power is more important than the good-will of the governed. Inversely, the governed can try to appeal to the foreign administration in order to oppose certain decisions of the traditional power. Either way the relation is distorted and the reciprocal obligations no longer seem clearly defined.

The economic, social and cultural transformations brought about by colonization have indirect consequences of the same kind. In his analysis of the political situation in the Soga country (Uganda), Fallers (1956) shows that the fall in the prestige of the chiefs is due to the conditional character of their power and to the weakening of their economic position. Inversely, he points out the social distance set up between the bureaucratized chiefs – who form 'an elite possessing a sub-culture of its own' – and the villagers: the autocratism resulting from the dysfunctioning of the traditional instruments that opposed the abuse of power became so strong that the colonial administration had to form 'official Councils' among the chiefs of various ranks. This example shows how misleading the formal permanences of the old political organization can be: only the chiefs of inferior rank, those at the head of village communities, remain in fact within the traditional model.

d. The incompatibility of the two systems of power and authority

Political anthropologists who claim their descent from the sociology of Weber see in the establishment of colonial power the origin of a process that effects the transition from the 'patrimonial' type of authority to the bureaucratic type. It is true that the colonial situation necessitates the coexistence of a strongly sacralized traditional system that regulates direct relations of subordination of a *personal* character and a modern system, based on the bureaucracy, that established less personalized relations. Although both are accepted – of necessity – as legitimate, their partial incompatibility remains. Fallers shows this, in relation to the Soga, when he points out the deviations and strategies to which the co-existence of the two systems, traditional and modern, gives rise: what is regarded as loyalty in the first becomes, because of the break in personal relations and old solidarities, nepotism in the second; moreover, subjects can now play a 'double game' by reference to either system according to circumstances and the interests involved. Beyond these observations, Fallers reveals the complex, composite aspect of the politico-administrative organization that functions during the colonial period. He shows the concurrent existence of three systems of government and administration: the one that is the result of colonization and another that is controlled by the traditional state are placed in a situation of relative incompatibility, while beneath both there remains the network of authority formed by the clans and lineages. The first two co-exist in a somewhat precarious manner, although the colonial administration attempts to 'rationalize', in the Weberian sense of the term, the mode of traditional government by bureaucratizing it and by bringing about a precise regulation of duties, taxes and tribute. The older clan system continues to put up the strongest resistance to the forces of change and appears, according to Fallers, as 'a major obstacle' whose disappearance is a condition of the success of all attempts at modernization.

e. The partial desacralization of power

All the consequences of colonization just considered combine to weaken the power and authority with which their holders were formerly invested. An additional and equally important cause must be considered. The desacralization of the offices of king and chief, even if the degree to which it has taken place varies according to circumstances, is still a determining factor. The power of the sovereign and chiefs is legitimized more by reference to the colonial government, which controls it and can contest it, than by reference to the ancient procedures, which have none the less survived. It no longer appears to have been received *only* by the consecration of the ancestors, deities or forces necessarily associated with the exercise of all power. K. Busia, in his study of the position of the chief in Ashanti (Ghana), shows that the decline in the practice of the traditional religion coincides with a loss in the power of the political authorities (1951). And events have shown – as in Rwanda in 1960 – that kings who still appear to be divinized can be overthrown.

It is a misleading paradox that the desacralization of political power also results from the intervention of imported and missionary religions which break the spiritual unity of which sovereigns or chiefs were the symbols, and often the guardians. Thus, by intervening in the same way as the bureaucracy, they assist in a laicization of the political sphere for which the peasant communities of Black Africa are ill prepared. This process helps us to understand the attempts that have been made by modern religious movements to re-sacralize political power through charismatic chiefs.

The characteristics that define the *immediate* political effects of modern colonization in Africa are to be found in other continents, even in countries that are better armed – by virtue of their history, their highly developed culture and technology – to resist colonial constraint. P. Mus (1952) suggests as much in his sociological analysis of the first Vietnam war. It was a case of a

political society that had been forced to submit to the vicissitudes of history, fashioned 'by conquest, resistance, conspiracy,
revolt and dissension throughout the centuries'. Mus describes
in meticulous detail the insidious struggle of the two systems of
government and administration, one monarchical, the other
colonial: the disappearance of villages and customary chiefs who
hide behind 'unrepresentative men' and the resistance of the
councils of notables, who are nevertheless manipulated by the
colonial power. He shows that the tutelage to which the traditional government is submitted is a trial that leads its subject
to doubt its ability, as the holder of the 'mandate of heaven', to
express 'the heavenly will', and thus leaves the way open to
rival authorities and to the possibility of profound changes.
Mus draws attention to the desacralization that disorientates
the peasantry and denatures the responsibility of the leaders:
'no State religion assuming responsibility both for the direction
of the Universe and the destiny of mankind' can now provide a
framework for peasant society; the conception of the world, like
the administration, is becoming secularized; the rulers no longer
assume responsibility for natural calamities by admitting that
they 'have fallen out of harmony with the Universe'. Active
political life -- that which is no longer content with sharing the
administration with the colonizers – then tends to express itself
by new means, which are not yet those of modern political
action; it is practised under cover of the traditions and within
the framework of the politico-religious sects that flourish by
establishing 'substitute religions' and by arousing 'a militant
attitude' among their adherents. This is, then, with greater historical depth and against a more complex cultural background,
the same combination of processes, but less obviously apparent,
as we found in the case of the African colonial situations. A
comparative analysis, bearing on other dependent societies,
would lead to the same results.

These tendencies are general in character, for they are an
expression of the direction of political change in most colonized
societies. However, because the traditional political systems are

very varied, we should be aware of the possibility that they may react *differently* to the experience of transformation begun by colonization. The ability of societies with or without a centralized state to adapt to imported administrative systems has often been regarded as a criterion that could serve as a basis for such an analysis. If we retain this distinction – which, in any case, is a dubious one in so far as the two forms of primitive political society are not radically different – it would seem that societies of the first type would be more easily receptive. This thesis can be justified by convergent arguments as well as by certain recent developments. 'Stateless' societies do not possess a rudimentary administration, involving an established hierarchy capable of opposing the modern bureaucracy, and for that reason are more liable to bureaucratization. They usually differentiate between the political and the religious roles, while in the case of societies with centralized political power the political and religious authorities are often linked, or even, as in the case of divine kingship, identical. Bureaucratic desacralization and laicization do not have, in those societies where the sacred preserves a large sphere of its own, the terrible effects feared by divine kings and their agents. Lastly, because egalitarian values have the ascendant over hierarchical values, though these are far from being ignored, the establishment of an administration that claims equality for all does not run counter to their fundamental cultural structure.*

These, then, are the data of any logical analysis. They must be confirmed by reference to findings in Africa. A comparison between the Gabonese Fang, with their ordered anarchy, and the Kongo, with their long tradition of a centralized government, showed their contrasting reactions to the same colonial situation. Around the 1940s, the Fang began a process of social reconstruction that led to a revitalization of the clan system. This was achieved by a revival of clan loyalties, by transforming the

* In 1959, the Rhodes–Livingstone Institute organized a symposium devoted to the theme *From Tribal Rule to Modern Government*. Cf. R. Apthorpe (1960).

villages and by establishing a bureaucracy in which a rough division of authority was made between the hierarchies and the colonial administrative system. They opposed colonialist domination while retaining certain modern methods introduced by colonization. The Kongo expressed a dual refusal and a dual opposition. Very early on, about 1920, they gave expression to their dissidence and tried to recover their autonomy. Their attempts at social reconstruction followed an original direction; they did not lead to a clan bureaucracy, but to the founding of indigenous churches that re-established the fundamental sacred links and to the creation of a new form of native power and newly functioning mechanisms of social integration. Because of these religious innovations, the Kongo were able to appear as the initiators of the nationalist movement and, with the full weight of these effective institutions behind them, to play an important part among the political forces freed by independence. They did not, like the Fang, adapt the model of the colonial administration to their projects for renewing their society, but rediscovered a form of response to the crisis resulting from colonization that had already been applied in the course of the history of the Kongo kingdom, notably at the beginning of the eighteenth century.*

The recent vicissitudes undergone by some of the traditional African states that still survive show that their modern adaptations must remain contained within narrow limits, beyond which the existence of the regime itself is threatened. In this respect, it is possible that very few present-day political societies would exemplify the type of 'modernizing autocracy' defined by Apter (1961). In Rwanda the challenge to royal power began in November 1959 with a peasant revolt that upset all the plans of 'progressive democratization' and led to the establishment of a Republic in 1961. In Buganda (Uganda), the incompatibility of the traditional power of the sovereign, within the framework of the kingdom, and the modern political authority, established at the level of the Ugandese state, was transformed into open antagonism, during the year 1966, on the occasion of

*Concerning this comparison, cf. Balandier (1963).

a grave political crisis, which concluded with a brief civil war that forced the king into flight and exile. In the same year, in Burundi, an attempt to modernize the monarchical system by their young heir to the throne failed very quickly and paved the way for the coup d'état that brought power to an army officer and led to a change of regime. One after the other the traditional states of the interlacustrian region in East Africa are being shaken and struck down; in the end, the process of modernization works against them.

These crises reveal not only the *immediate* political consequences of colonization and decolonization, but also their *indirect* political effects. In Rwanda, the overthrow of a monarchy that had been established for several centuries was preceded by a confrontation of the two great, but unequal constitutive groups: the peasant majority opposed the aristocracy, first by demanding 'internal decolonization', then by passing from insubordination to violence. A class struggle, of a rudimentary kind, was made possible by the social and cultural transformations introduced by colonization; the rejection of the traditional power and its agents results from the rejection of the basic inequality that characterized the old society of Rwanda. And this dual contestation has facilitated the adhesion of the peasants to the modern, bureaucratic system of government.

The process of modernization, which was set in train by the colonial adventure, affects political action and its organizations *indirectly* through changes in social stratifications. It sets up the generators of social classes formed outside the narrow ethnic framework. In Black Africa five social strata can usually be differentiated during the colonial period. They are both distinct – often even named – and ordered, and they classify the agents of the colonial power from the point of view of its political and economic forms: the agents of westernization (the 'literate elites'), the rich planters, the tradespeople and small capitalists, and lastly the wage earners, organized (or not) in professional groups. 'Certain of these social strata tend to form alliances based on common interests and to arouse, through

reaction, the self-awareness of the most under-privileged group –
the last. Thus the outlines are formed of a bureaucratic bourgeoisie, an economic bourgeoisie and an as yet quite small
proletariat' (Balandier, 1965a). The colonial situation directs
this dynamic in two ways: by discouraging the formation of
social classes and by encouraging, when the demand for autonomy becomes vocal and organized, the formation of an opposition 'front' that limits the antagonisms between the emergent
classes. Once independence has been achieved it causes a thaw
in political life, for it creates the conditions most favourable to
the appearance of classes and makes possible the sharpening of
the struggle for power. Yet the situation does not become more
simplified. It is still characterized by economic backwardness
and economic dependence, which tend to contradict the differentiation of the social classes. Moreover, the relations of production (even the most modern ones) have not yet acquired in
Black Africa the determining role they have in 'Western'
societies. The explanation for this lies in the political situation –
at the level of the relations that exist with the new power; the
establishment of this power – and the struggles that it gives rise
to – help to strengthen the only fully formed class, the ruling
class. It is participation in the exercise of political power that
gives economic power, rather than the reverse. In this respect,
the young national state and the traditional state have a similar
effect, since position in relation to the state apparatus still determines social status, the form of the relation to the economy and
material power.

In South-East Asia similar transformations have taken place.
The example of Burma – which colonialism robbed not only of
its independence, but also, in 1885, of its traditional form of
government – is one of the most revealing. The direct political
consequences of colonization were brutal: the elimination of
the Burmese monarchy and the introduction into the country
of the administrative system already established in India; the
displacement of the Burmese, who had become the dominant
ethnic group, to the advantage of other ethnic groups and

'minorities'; the desacralization of political life by the application of the principle of the separation of church and state; the denaturation of the politico-administrative units by changes to their frontiers and the establishment of a colonial administration; the decline of the mechanisms of conciliation and of the traditional courts of justice. Burma is an extreme case of the process already described. The country was subjected to a double colonization: that of the British *and* that of their many agents, brought in from India, who retarded the introduction into the country of modern administrative and economic methods. At the time of independence in 1948 only a small percentage of the senior civil servants were Burmese. However, the colonial period did see the formation of a new social stratification that was partly dissociated from ethnic boundaries. A social stratum, limited in size and recruited above all from the formerly dominant ethnic group, developed within the administration and the army. The native wage-earning class developed slowly, in competition with labour brought in from India. But it was in the agricultural sector that the most important changes occurred, for the colonizers completely overthrew the system of traditional land rights: they set up land ownership, encouraged the transfer of land and established the practice of mortgage. Moreover, because of the unequal economic development of the country, differences in rentals appeared and widened to the advantage of the delta region. A social stratum embracing the landowners, some of whom were absentee landowners, and the moneylenders gradually widened and was joined by the small group of native 'contractors'.

At independence, the unity resulting from the opposition to the colonizers was broken. Internal splits and antagonisms became clearly apparent: between ethnic groups that were unequally prepared for modernization; between the traditional powers (diminished, but not abolished) and the modern power; between the developing social classes. Large areas remained outside the control of the new government; the political machinery soon broke down and bureaucratic positions were used for personal gain. Ten years after independence, in 1958, the army seized power for a brief period with a view to 'restoring order'. The modern political system had not yet found its balance. The peasantry, which remained divided by its ethnic differences, remained unenthusiastic about a distant and little understood power. The emergent working class and the industrial bourgeoisie, though numerically weak, tried to increase their pressure on the state, while the ruling class became more clearly apparent during the ensuing struggles. The effects of colonization and decolonization worked in the same direction: the first had diminished the old powers too much for them to be capable of being given a modernist form; the second had been incapable of initiating, across the ethnic boundaries, and with sufficient intensity, the changes that would make the new social stratification the *only* generator of modern political activity (cf. Hagen, 1964, pp. 432–70, 540).

Without adding any further example or analyses of concrete situations, attention should now be focused on the various attempts to give a theoretical treatment of the problem of the relations between the dynamic of social stratifications and the dynamic of political modernization. One of the most recent attempts of this kind is that of Apter in his work, *The Politics of Modernization*, published in 1965. Apter sets out with the declaration that the most direct effect of modernization is the emergence of new social roles: to the accepted traditional roles are added 'adaptive' roles, created by a partial transformation of some of the traditional ones, and 'innovatory' roles; these three types of roles are in varying degrees incompatible. In addition, Apter distinguishes three forms of social stratification that frequently coexist in societies that have embarked on a course of modernization: the caste system (in the widest sense, for it can be recognized in societies with *separate* races and cultures), the class system and the system of statutory hierarchies within which there is vigorous competition between individuals. The three types of role can be seen in operation in each of the three systems of stratification, and conflicts may arise between roles within the same category of social stratification, between similar roles from one category to another and finally between groups formed according to these three categories. These conflicts express divergent interests and oppositions between values. As soon as they increase in intensity, a resolution of them is sought at the political level, either within a regime that regulates the competition between the various roles, or within a regime that operates by means of elimination and by bringing about a total and drastic reorganization of society.

According to the terminology worked out by Apter, the first solution is characteristic of the 'reconciliation system', the second of the 'mobilization system'. In the second case the economy is subjected to the state apparatus, the single party becomes the instrument of modernization, social roles and social stratification are the object of a policy of radical transformation; China, engaged in successive revolutions since 1949 – the 'cultural revolution' being the most constricting – provides an extreme illustration of this type. In the 'reconciliation system', even though the diversity of roles and modes of stratification is maintained, the enlargement of the 'modern sector' is brought about by means of political action, the economy and education. The groups remain in open competition and the variations of social stratification result from the degrees of pressure they exert on the state power. The system is thus threatened by corruption, which favours the formation of 'clienteles', by stagnation or political instability. Closer to this type than to the preceding one are the systems of 'modernizing autocracy' – of which the most frequent form is the military oligarchy (Apter, 1965, chapters. 1, 2, 4).

Apter's analysis, especially as applied to the transitional situations that follow the colonial situation, seems vulnerable in so far as it takes insufficient account of the recurrent effects of colonialism and applies over-simplified models. Moreover, it does not examine systematically the dynamic of the relations between tradition and modernity, by means of which, however, a number of analogies emerge. In the traditional societies, in which the economic determinisms are relatively weak, the hierarchies and social roles are primarily influenced by other factors, notably political and religious ones; their more or less precarious adjustment usually operates on the political plane. In societies undergoing modernization, the preponderance of the political remains accentuated – and for two obvious reasons: the politico-administrative structure is set up, at national level, well before the modern economy can be developed, and it acts as the principal instrument linking the many different social groups and strata. This similarity of situation partly explains the possibility of transferring certain 'political models' from traditional to modern sectors. It also reveals – as Apter emphasizes – that the political apparatus may, during the process of modernization, continue to determine the principal forms of social stratification that remain in reciprocal relation with the system of government to which they are linked.

2. The Dynamic of Traditionalism and Modernity

Recent research has questioned the characteristics usually attributed to traditional systems and traditionalism. Most of this research is in the field of political anthropology and is based on a refusal to identify tradition with 'fixism' and an attempt to uncover the 'dynamic aspects' of the traditional society. Although processes may hinder change and innovation can only be introduced on the basis of existing forms and established values, this society is not condemned to being a mere prisoner of its past.

The notion of traditionalism remains imprecise. It is seen as *continuity*, whereas modernity involves break. It is usually defined as conformity to *timeless* norms, those affirmed or justified by myth or dominant ideology and those handed down by tradition through a variety of procedures. This definition has no scientific force. In fact, the notion can be given greater rigour only if one differentiates between the various *present-day* expressions of traditionalism. The first of these expressions – and the one closest to the current use of the term – corresponds to a fundamental traditionalism, an attempt to safeguard the values and the social and cultural arrangements most hallowed by the past. In Indian society the perenniality of the caste system and of the ideology that expresses it reveals, despite the ambiguous and varied relations that link it to modernity, this force of conservation; in fact, although changes do occur within the system, the system does not change as a whole, for to do so would subject the entire social structure of rural India to the attacks of change (cf. Dumont, 1966). *Formal traditionalism* usually coexists with the preceding type. It is defined by the maintenance of institutions and of social or cultural structures, the content of which is modified; only certain means are preserved from the past – the functions and aims have changed. The study of the African cities that sprang from the establishment of colonies in the southern Sahara has shown that traditional models have been transferred into an urban environment in order to establish a minimum of order in a new, developing society. During the period of colonial domination, the *traditionalism of resistance* served as a protective screen or camouflage to conceal reactions of refusal; the essentially different character of the dominated culture gave it, in the eyes of the colonizers, a strange, incomprehensible quality; traditions, either modified or revived, served as a defence for expressions of opposition and for attempts to break the ties of dependence. This process operated most frequently on the religious plane: the traditional representation of the sacred masked modern political expressions. After the colonial period, a new phenomenon appears that might be called *pseudo-traditionalism*. In such cases, manipulated tradition becomes a way of giving meaning to the new realities, or to expressing a demand by expressing a disagreement with the modernist leaders.

This form of traditionalism requires a more advanced analysis and an illustration. A recent study by J. Favret (1967) devoted to the two post-independence rural movements in Algeria

provides a significant example in this respect. The peasants of
the Aurès, who have inherited an 'anti-state tradition', are
familiar with a state of insurrection – *siba* – which has frequently
expressed a refusal on the part of their 'segmentary' communities to be subjected to the central power. Their demands
for independent government operate, in a sense, in reverse:
they protest against under-administration and the slowness
of the spread of the instruments and signs of modernity in
their region. With this end in view, they revive traditional political mechanisms. By wishing to force the authorities into taking
action that would reduce the gap between their desire for progress and the means at their disposal, they rebel 'through an
excess of modernity'. Hamlets secede by breaking off relations
with the administration, and dissident personalities – seen as
fighters for the faith, *mujahidin* – use violence 'in order to draw
the attention of the state' by the only means at their disposal.
In such a case, traditionalism is revived as a weapon in the service of ends that are the opposite of tradition. In Kabylia, where
maquis groups and local powers were organized during the
months following independence the situation was very different;
pseudo-traditionalism fulfilled a function that might be called
semantic, since it gives meaning to the new political forms. In the
event, it was not merely a question of satisfying Kabyl separat-
ism and the Berber democratic spirit. The peasants, who were
incapable as yet of conceiving in what way they belonged to an
abstract state devoid of historical traditions, brought about a
revival of the old political relations. They used these relations
as a means of gaining a better understanding with the modern
state and to put pressure upon it; their political elites could
therefore organize an insurrection and influence the decisions
of the Algerian government. In fact, traditionalism does
not reveal the survival of primordial groups, but it gives
them 'a reactional existence'; they have less significance in
themselves than in reference to the situation created after
independence.

  This simplified typology is an inadequate account of the

dynamic of traditionalism and modernity. A general process must be envisaged: the political structures resulting from the establishment of the 'new states' can be interpreted, during the transitional period, only *in the terms of the old language*. These structures can command neither immediate comprehension nor immediate support from the traditional peasantries. This situation, which explains the revival of political groups, behaviour and symbols that were disappearing, tends to increase the incompatibilities between the separatist factors (racial, ethnic, regional, cultural, religious) and the unitary factors conditioning the national constitution, the functioning of the state and the expansion of 'modernist' civilization. Most of the poor, developing countries have undergone or are undergoing the consequences of these incompatibilities.

An example is to be found in Indonesia, which possesses regional diversities – accentuated by its insular character and the supremacy of Java – and religious, cultural and ethnic variations. Although post-colonial policy has attempted to create a balance between the different forces, in particular by exalting 'revolutionary solidarity', the ideologies that have been developed have all been syncretic in character, even that of the Indonesian Communists who have combined a simplified Marxism with traditional cultural themes. The balance could not be maintained however; from 1957 onwards, there was an increase in regional rebellion and the new power gradually declined. C. Geertz sees this process as a chain reaction. Each step in the direction of modernity has caused a retrenchment of the separatisms that have put increasing pressure on the central power and furnished further evidence of its weakness. Each instance of its powerlessness has increased instability and induced institutional experiments and frequent changes of ideology (Geertz, 1963). Two contrary movements, then, have operated in synchronization: on the one hand, a revival of political initiative at regional level, supported by traditional elements; on the other, a gradual loss of control over public affairs that has discredited the central government and created a state of inflation as regards modernist organization, ideologies and symbols. The breaking-point was reached in 1965 and culminated in the seizure of power by the Army. Political struggles are to a large degree, though not exclusively, expressed *in terms of* the debate between the traditional and the modern; this debate is really their means and not their main cause.

At the level of continental-sized nations (the Indian Union) or of the continent whose division into nations is a result above all of colonial divisions (Africa), this debate has an importance reminiscent, for the peasantries, of the play of fate. It could be said of India that it is 'a labyrinth of social and cultural structures', that it experiences all the 'primordial conflicts' caused by the incompatibility of the many (reactivated) traditional social relations and the new relations brought about by the economic and political transformations. In Black Africa, the discords are equally apparent, especially as the instability of the political regimes contrasts with the permanence of the use of traditional models in the villages. The Black nations are in the process of creating themselves and are not yet formed. The integration of the various ethnic groups often remains precarious, so much so that the break up of the larger states – such as Congo-Kinshasa and Nigeria – remains a constant threat. The result of this situation is that the parties and their tendencies, the movements, even when termed revolutionary, express as much the relative weight of the ethnic groups as the variety of options as to the structures of the nation and its economy. Such a state of affairs has scarcely been altered by the single-party system: the elimination of confrontation has not abolished the obligation to divide power according to ethnic, religious or regional categories. Independence gave a new dynamic to tradition, according to a double orientation. On the one hand, it freed the forces that had been suppressed during the colonial period, as can be seen in several of the crises that have occurred in recent years – crises which reveal a resurgence of tribal and/or religious antagonisms. On the other, modern political activity has been unable to organize and express itself except by means of a kind of *translation*: the traditional models and symbols become once more the means of communication and explanation by which the leaders address the Black peasants. One of these 'permanent' facts seems even more fundamental. The old conceptions of power have not all been effaced, especially in regions where vigorous states have arisen at various moments in history. Thus, in the Congo, the image of the president appears, in a certain way, as the reflection of the figure of the traditional sovereign – in particular, that of the king of Kongo. The chief must manifest his power, literally seize the throne, and hold on to power by force in the interest of the collectivity. From this point of view, the recent struggles for the control of the state apparatus are only a present-day version of the 'wars of succession' and the military power is still recognized as the best armed. To the person of the *strong* chief is associated that of the *just* chief, respected for his wisdom, capable of being the supreme arbiter, of imposing respect for the law and of enforcing his conciliatory decisions. A third figure is associated with these two in the representation of kingship: that of the *charismatic* chief, possessing a special relationship with the people, the country and the system of forces that regulate fertility and prosperity. Power is still conceived in terms of the triple aspect of power, arbitration and the sacred. Since 1960 the Congo has failed to unite in one person these three figures of the chief; according to the traditional notions, this situation would largely explain its present state of weakness.

The research now being conducted under the name of political anthropology is only beginning to consider the various modalities of the relation between tradition and modernity. It can no longer be content with general or approximate appreciations and must therefore determine unities and levels of inquiry in which analysis would be capable of attaining an increasing scientific efficacity.

a. The village community

It constitutes a society in little, with definite frontiers, in which
the confrontation of the traditional and the modern, the sacral
and the historical, are clearly apparent. Within its boundaries
radical transformations are taking place, not without resistance
and misunderstanding, and, for this very reason the researches
concerning them are most instructive. G. Althabe (1968) has
devoted a study, based on meticulous and patient observations,
of the villages of the Betsimisaraka people, in the eastern coastal
region of Madagascar. In particular, his analysis shows how
difficult it was for the village powers to adapt to the administrative system introduced by the new Malagasy State. Within
these communities, a split has appeared between the world of
internal life, dominated by tradition, and the world of external
life, the many relations now established with 'the outside
world', in which the agents and forces of modernity operate.
This dualism is expressed in a quite physical way in the arrangement of the village area. The fields where mountain rice is
grown, situated at some distance from the dwellings, constitute
the area dominated by tradition; the practices they require and
the system of symbols that they sustain conform to the traditional requirements still denoted by the term *tavy*. The village
agglomeration, situated on the road, open to the representatives of the administration and to external trade, full of imported objects and symbols, has become the attack front of
modernism. The dualism also finds expression in the practices
that regulate community life and in the settlement of the differences that arise within it. If it is an internal matter, the old
hierarchies are appealed to and respected, and meetings for
discussion (and decision) conform to traditional principles. If it
is an external matter, particularly one concerning relations with
the representatives of the state, very different rules are applied;
the meetings do not reveal the fundamental social relations and
do not provide an occasion for the community to reveal the order

that defines its structure. In the first case, social relations try to preserve their richness and symbolic efficacity; in the second, they have an improvised quality and are in fact based on foreign models – inherited from the colonizers – and, for that reason, partially challenged. The factors of modernity are generally regarded as being external to village society.

Although the Betsimisaraka peasant seems to live on two levels, a deeper study shows that the reality of the situation is not so simple. A new institution, borrowed from neighbouring groups and adapted, has spread a good deal in recent years; this is a ritual associated with possession by identified and hierarchized spirits, the *tromba*. Its significance cannot be confined to the religious sphere, for the relation with the sacred lends support, in this case, to the new, emergent social and cultural order. This ritual, which is reminiscent of a community experiment, has a syncretic character in the sense that it creates a combination of modern elements and symbols and traditional elements and symbols. At the same time it expresses a double negation: it rejects certain traditional aspects – those that seem most devoid of life – by challenging the cult of the ancestors, in its old form, and the techniques of divination; it rejects the methods of modernism that are recognized as foreign, by expressing itself as a counter-Christianity and by establishing new relations of dependence and authority. The *tromba* provides an exceptionally fruitful field for observation and analysis. It shows that the man living in 'dualist' societies does not organize his existence by facing alternatively two separate sectors, one regulated by tradition, the other by modernity. It makes it possible to grasp, through lived experience, the dialectic that operates between a traditional (declining) system and a modern system (imposed from outside); from this dialectic emerges a third, unstable type of socio-cultural system whose origin is to be found in the confrontation of the first two. The interpretation of these phenomena runs counter to the banal theories of sociological dualism. Because of its very size, the village community is the unit where this complex dynamic is best seen at work, where the new structures can be seen in their emergent state and where modern political action is expressed in the most immediate way.

In all its geographical extent the work of the anthropologists shows that this statement is of general application when it is a matter of analysing the effects of modernizing forces on the traditional order. The many studies devoted to Indian villages are the most revealing, particularly at the level of political anthropology. They reveal 'the recent changes introduced by the inclusion of the village in an economic and political whole that exerts a strong influence upon it', the increase in the causes of friction, which exacerbates the hostile relations between 'factions', and the decline in the effectiveness of the '*panchaya*' – the assembly that exercises authority and arbitration.* All this research shows, through the complexity of the order with which it is dealing, the vanity of premature and trivializing generalizations. Caution is all the more imperative when societies that have undergone revolutionary changes – as is the case in the Chinese countryside – are being studied. In fact, tradition cannot be completely eliminated and certain of its elements survive in a different form: it then becomes even more difficult to decipher traditional elements (cf. Myrdal, 1964).

The village communities are the most relevant *research units*, for it is at the level of the village that the confrontation between tradition and modernity takes place. We must now consider by what *means* modernity acts upon the political sphere: its instruments, its arguments and its justifications. The political party must be regarded as a factor of modernization, while the function of ideology and the transition from backward-looking myth to forward-looking modern ideology must be examined in greater detail.

*Cf. the bibliographical notes and suggestions of Dumont (1966, sections 74, 75, 84).

b. The political party as a modernizing instrument

In traditional societies that are in the course of transformation, the party fulfils a number of different functions: it defines the new or renewed state, directs the national economy, organizes the supremacy of the political and helps to reshape the social structures. This participation in change is all the more active in so far as the rule of the single party or 'national movement', which was general in the years following independence, is widely predominant. The political party is the primary means of modernization by virtue of its origin in the initiative of the modernist elites, its organization, which gives it a closer contact with the community than that possessed by the administration, and lastly its functions and aims, since it wishes to be, and in various fields is, the motive force behind economic development. These aspects are accentuated in the case of unitary parties or movements that result 'from a desire to change the community, to restructure social relations and to engender a new form of consciousness and ethics'; in putting forward this definition, Apter (1965, chapter 6) characterizes the 'system of mobilization' that organizes the drastic modification of society.

But the dynamic of tradition and modernity is always present in the operations of the political party and the first cannot be regarded simply as an obstacle to the progress of the second. The party is often formed from 'intermediary groups', expressing modern aims in traditional forms and symbols: tribal associations, cultural movements, syncretic churches. In western Nigeria, among the Yoruba, an association founded in 1945 and honouring the founding ancestor (*Oduduwa*) by promoting Yoruba values and culture, was instrumental in reviving political activity and lent its support to the 'Action Group' party. In the Ivory Coast, the 'African Democratic Union' was born from an association of planters – therefore modernist peasants – and used as links the initiation societies – notably the most widespread, that of the *Poro* – to establish itself. In both Congo

States the religious movements born from syncretism, from the wish to restore order in the domain of the sacred, and the cultural associations, have been the major base of modern political life.

Tradition, which affected the parties at the time of their birth, continues to exert its influence on their structures and means of expression. The parties wish to construct a unitary framework over and above the various separatisms, to ensure the spread of new ideas, to give a preponderant role to their agents of modernity, but their introduction into a peasant environment obliges them to make concessions to the older order. They must establish local alliances with the traditional elders, the religious authorities and the leaders of various semi-modernist organizations. In Indonesia a specific term (*aliran* = stream) denotes the various social currents that must be canalized in this way. Although the parties use the most obvious instruments of modernity – the various mass media of information and persuasion, the bureaucratic apparatus – they are forced to adapt their language and symbolism to the traditional environment upon which they wish to act. They are condemned to cultural ambiguity during the initial period, and often beyond it. By reviving old and effective symbols, they organize the ceremonial of political life (sometimes incorporating ritual elements as well) in order to sacralize it, they give their leader a double face or mould a heroic personality for him (if necessary by placing him in the line of popular heroes) and, lastly, they employ traditional means to enforce party membership and establish the authority of their agents. Their doctrines and ideologies are largely syncretic. M. Halpern has drawn attention to the existence in certain Muslim countries of a mixture of opposed traditions: Marxist philosophy is presented as the replica, in the modern world and on the material plane, of the traditional Islamic philosophy; each on its own level is regarded as having ushered in a new order (Halpern, 1963). The critical study of the various specific forms of socialism in the developing countries – and particularly 'African socialism' – also shows them to be syncretisms. Omnipresent tradition imposes limits on the modernizing activity of the political party that the most radical policies fail to erode except with the passage of time.

c. Ideology, an expression of modernity

The political function of ideologies is stimulated during revolutionary periods and during phases of profound change in societies and their cultures. In the case of certain traditional societies in mutation, such as those of Black Africa, this function is all the more evident in that the political ideology appeared with the modern period, over the ruins of the myths that upheld the old order.

The ideologies associated with the plans for national construction (or reconstruction) and with the enterprises of economic development and modernization have certain features in common. They are marked by reactions to the situation of dependence: the condemnation of exploitation and oppression and the exaltation of independence are their major themes. These themes are all the more effective in that they help to explain technological and economic backwardness. In so far as they are determined by the need for the unity of the nation to prevail over the various kinds of separatisms, there is a predominance of unitary themes and symbols: the personality of the national leader is sacralized (he may even be regarded as a saviour) and the nation itself becomes the object of nothing less than a political religion. Moreover, these ideologies must assist in a psychological conversion that has been called a 'new deal of the emotions'. They are presented in two versions: a more complicated one intended for the political and intellectual elites and for diffusion abroad and a more simplified version, couched in traditional vocabulary, aimed at the peasantry and those social strata less affected by modern education. Lastly, these ideologies are largely inspired by social philosophies and political doctrines developed outside the country in question. This is the case with socialism and Marxism and with certain forms of nationalism. This 'foreignness' often gives ideology a *syncretic* character that is apparent in the definition of most specific forms of socialism. It is also at the root of a contradiction that is difficult to overcome: modern political thought is fashioned with foreign intellectual tools, but these tools are used to further 'nationalist' development and often a defence of specificity. J. Berque, in his study of 'the Arabs from yesterday to tomorrow', has interpreted this effort 'to adjust to others while remaining true to oneself', this 'contradictory need' which explains how the demand for modernity is not a total negation of tradition (1960, chapters 1, 12, 13).

Modernist ideologies are also characterized by their instability, by their own movement, in relation to the transformations achieved and the degree of change in political consciousness. They vary in so far as they relate to societies and cultures that have been subjected to rapid change and remain significant only for a relatively short time. Apter has tried to determine the cycle of their formation and the sequence of their variations (1965, pp. 314–27). At first, the ideology is diffused and linked with multiple and, to a large extent, contradictory images. Then, under pressure from necessity and events, it is built up and new elements are added to it, as soon as its recipients become receptive to the themes and symbols that have no part in tradition. At its highest point – corresponding with its point of maximum effectiveness – the ideology takes on a utopian and millennium-oriented aspect: it exalts the society of the future and confers on the collective enterprise an immediate efficacity and a universal historical significance – for example, the mission of realizing the only authentic revolution. At the end of the process, the ideology declines; the militants have become managers and the force of circumstance leads to a practical realism, to the development of an ideological system strongly marked by pragmatism.

These ideologies of modernization are not yet imposed by radical innovation: they are too mobile and too circumstantial. Their analysis seems disappointing and often repetitive. Never the less, they provide political anthropology with a field of investigation rich in unsolved problems, in that they make it possible to grasp the structure of tradition and the similarity that exists between them and the myths of tradition. In this respect, the African countries offer the most revealing examples. As soon as the national movements take shape, a political ideology is formed, with the support of the mythical themes of revolt or resistance that appeared during the colonial period. Originally the initiative belonged to an intellectual minority that was anxious to promote a cultural as well as a political liberation. The most representative ideology of this phase is the 'theory of negritude', developed by French-speaking Africans, then given philosophical form by Sartre. As a footnote to our main theme we should place the ideological work of essayists who wish to put African history to militant use. They treat the past in such a way as to assure the rehabilitation of the Negro peoples and cultures. They invert the relation of dependence and transform the recognized civilizations into dependents of an unknown African civilization. The essentially political ideologies – the more recent ones – possess a messianic quality, a sort of theoretical reflection of the popular messianic movements that expressed the first organized opposition to colonialism. Thus the founders of African socialism not only have a responsibility to proceed with an adaptation that is regarded as necessary, but also the certainty of contributing to the salvation of socialism by enriching it with their own fertilizing values (Balandier, 1962).

This, then, is the path that has led from the traditional myth, with its partial ideological content, to the modern political ideologies and doctrines, which still contain a good deal of myth. This development from the myth with ideological implications to the modern systems of thought with mythical implications leads us to *the* problem facing all old societies undergoing change. This problem is that of the permanent dialectic between tradition and revolution.

Conclusion

Perspectives of
Political Anthropology

Political anthropology is developing at the very moment when the anthropological approach is being questioned: the objects to which that approach are mainly applied – archaic or traditional societies – are undergoing radical changes; the methods and theories that have defined the approach since before the Second World War are being subjected to a critical evaluation that is bringing about a renewal of the discipline. Political anthropology, then, is a new configuration emerging within a highly disturbed scientific field. Max Gluckman and Fred Eggan consider that it was virtually founded when the collective work entitled *African Political Systems* appeared in 1940; since that date research has been carried out in a great many fields and a good deal of theoretical thought has resulted. Two recent publications have proved its vitality and the rigour of its methods: *Political Systems and the Distribution of Power* (A.S.A., 1965a) examines a particular problem, that of power and the strategies it implies, and *Political Anthropology* (Schwartz, Turner and Tuden, 1966) is a collection of texts that reveals some of the major directions being taken in the discipline.

But this late specialization of anthropology is really more a project in the course of achievement than an already fully developed field. At first it suffered from an ambiguous situation; it remained so marginal that anthropologists did not regard politics as one of their major preoccupations, but considered it practically as one aspect of a derived system of relations whose *primary* expression was social and/or religious; it developed outside the older political disciplines – challenging them under the form of political philosophy or political science, which remained for a long time confined within its 'western provincialism'. But its own development led it to occupy a central position, one which made it possible to study politics in all its diversity and to create the conditions for a broader comparative study. This development forced it to draw closer to its parent disciplines. The works published during the last fifteen years show these external influences: in the first place, that of Weber, which is particularly preponderant in the case of American and British researchers; then, that of contemporary political scientists, notably Easton, the author of a study published in 1953 under the title, *The Political System*.

This moving together of the different disciplines has provoked confrontation and criticism. Easton criticizes political anthropologists for concerning themselves with an ill-defined object and for not having clearly differentiated the aspects, structures and political behaviour of the other manifestations of social life. He accuses them of failing to grasp politics in its essence and specificity. The criticism has some substance, but it seems useful to recall that the societies under study do not always possess a distinct political organization and that the political scientists themselves have not always clearly defined the political order. Easton observes, moreover, that political anthropology operates without having fixed its main theoretical principles (1959, pp. 210–47). The research carried out in recent years has done much to invalidate this criticism, apart from the fact that the theoretical risks taken by the precursors of the discipline have encouraged greater prudence. One cannot reproach a scientific discipline for the very thing that constitutes its vulnerability. But one positive element at least remains incontestable: political anthropology has led to a *decentralization*, for it has universalized thought – extending it to Pygmy and Amerindian groups that have a minimum of central power – and broken the spell that the state has long exerted on political theorists. This achievement is regarded as being so important that Parkinson – a recognized and celebrated political scientist –

has suggested that the comparative study of the systems of political theories should be entrusted to anthropologists.

It would be puerile to be content with this flattering suggestion. A more detailed examination of the question is necessary. Through its scientific practice and the results that it has achieved, political anthropology exerts an influence on the mother discipline from which it was formed. Its mere existence gives it *a critical efficacity* in relation to that discipline. It helps to alter the usual images of the societies examined by the anthropologists. These societies can no longer be seen as unanimist societies – possessing a mechanically obtained consensus – and as balanced systems, scarcely affected by entropy. A study of their politics leads to an apprehension of each of these societies in terms of its everyday life, its activities and its problems, over and above the appearances it presents to the observer and the theories it can give rise to. Social arrangements are seen to be approximate, struggle and dispute (direct or covert) ever present. Because it operates on *an essentially dynamic reality*, political anthropology must take into account the internal dynamic of so-called 'traditional' societies; it complements the logical analysis of positions by the logical analysis of oppositions – and reveals a necessary connexion between these two approaches. Indeed, it is remarkable that terms such as 'strategy' and 'manipulation' are being increasingly used. The argument is a minor one. The conclusions drawn by Leach from an excellent study in political anthropology are more demonstrative (1964). Taking the case of the Kachin of Burma, he draws attention to the instability of the real systems and to the dynamisms operating within them; he clearly shows the multiplicity of the models used by the Kachin, according to circumstances – indeed, so varied are these models that their conceptual apparatus can encompass the expression of contrary aspirations and the affirmation of contradictory legitimacies; he shows that the balance is to be found in the model (as created by the society itself or as constructed by the anthropologist), and not in facts. Leach, too, shows that the dynamism is *inherent in the structure* and that it is expressed not only by change – a view of social reality that we formulated some fifteen years ago in an attempt to analyse its theoretical and methodological implications. A growing number of political anthropologists now share this interpretation. Gluckman has recently come closer to the same interpretation: he uses the notion of 'oscillating equilibrium' to interpret the dynamic of certain traditional African states, thus lending greater flexibility to a hitherto too static concept (1965).

Political anthropology is renewing the old debate concerning the relation of traditional (or archaic) societies to history. One of the principal reasons for this has already been mentioned: it is in the political sphere that history leaves its strongest imprint. If the so-called 'segmentary' societies belong to history by their movement of successive composition and decomposition, by the changes made in their religious systems and by their openness (either willingly or under constraint) to outside influences, the societies with strong, centralized government belong to history in a different way – wholly and completely. They belong to a history richer in determining events, and they reveal a greater awareness of the possibilities of acting upon social reality. The state is born out of political events, is itself the creator of political events and accentuates the inequalities that generate imbalance and change. From the moment the state emerges, the anthropological method can no longer avoid an encounter with history. It can no longer be conducted as if the history of the traditional societies were near the state of zero: a mere repetition. It is the anthropologists concerned with the study of state systems who have contributed most to this recognition of history, and to showing the political use of the data of ideological history. Most of this work has been done in the field of Africanist studies – in Nupe (Nadel), in Buganda (Apter and Fallers), in former Rwanda (Vansina), in Kongo (Balandier) and in the Nguni kingdoms of southern Africa (Gluckman). Through this work a new – more *dynamic* – anthropological theory is developing. It is significant that Luc de Heusch's latest work, on Rwanda, which belongs to the same historical and cultural configuration as the states of the eastern inter-lacustrian region, is presented as a 'structural and historical analysis'. The second aspect of the approach corrects the in-adequacies and deviations of the first (de Heusch, 1966).

It should also be said that political anthropology leads to a more critical consideration of the ideological systems by which traditional societies explain themselves and justify their specific order. Even Malinowski saw myth as a charter that regulated social practice – and thus helped to maintain existing modes of distributing power, property and privilege. According to this interpretation, myth encourages conformity and works in the interests of the established power, either to protect it against potential threats or to provide a basis for the periodic rituals that maintain its force. The most recent interpretations, based on new research, often emphasize the political significance of myth. They reveal the elements of political theory that myth conceals: Beattie has developed this method of interpretation – and demonstrated its scientific interest – by applying it to the case of the Nyoro of Uganda. They reveal the ideology – favour-able to the holders of power and to the aristocracies – implied in myth and certain other 'traditions': Vansina observes that in traditional Rwanda the traditions are all altered to favour the dominant 'caste' and that this process of alteration accelerates with time. The ideology is unmasked when the inegalitarian order seems safely ensconced; its manipulators no longer feel constrained to adopt more subtle methods.

Leach offers a general interpretation of the myths that makes it possible to uncover their political meanings and functions. According to him, myths integrate the contradictions that man must confront, from the most existential to those resulting from social practice; their function is to attenuate these contradic-tions and make them bearable. This aim is achieved only by the regrouping of mythical narratives possessing similarities and differences, and not by citing isolated myths; far from resolving the contradiction, the confusion of the different versions serves to *mask* it. Leach, who had already developed this mode of elucidating myths in his study of Kachin political systems, has recently applied it to the problem presented by the legitimacy of Solomon's power. He shows that the Biblical text is contradictory, but arranged in such a way that Solomon always remains the legitimate inheritor of power. Sovereignty is justified by conquest; it fulfils the divine promise given to the Israelites (Leach, 1966).*

Political anthropology exercises a wider critical function. It emphasizes certain of the difficulties inherent in the dominant theories and in the methodology of the anthropologists; it is confronted by these difficulties and reveals them. The functionalist method, which was used in the first series of studies of primitive governments, led to an impasse. This method sought to detect the principles that lay behind the functioning of the political systems, without really determining what these systems were, while conferring on the notion that described them an absolute value that is now contested. It proposed to define the functions of politics – to found and/or maintain the social order and to guarantee security – but its nature was never elucidated. Indeed, a good deal of work has been devoted to an inadequately identified object. The authors of *African Political Systems* are not immune from this criticism, although their work has always been regarded as an admirable reference. Functionalist analyses have also failed to recognize the full scope of the political sphere – usually confining it to the *internal* relations enforced by the state – and its specificity – regarding it as a system of well articulated relations, similar to organic or mechanical systems. Recent theoretical work sees it as the bearer of poorly integrated elements, exposed to tensions and antagonisms, affected by the strategies of individuals or groups and the play of contestations. Its essentially dynamic character, like that of any 'social field', is now better recognized. Lastly, functionalism rejected history and a consideration of the effects of time, for

---

*D. Sperber (1967) has shown the scope of this analysis in an article entitled 'Edmund Leach et les anthropologues'.

they deprived social systems of their apparent stability and equilibrium; A. L. Kroeber has made a vigorous attack on this front, though without achieving a final victory. For political processes take place in time: this statement may be tautologous, but this has not prevented it from being widely ignored. The latest methods strive to retain its full implications. The editors of the collective work *Political Anthropology* remind us that 'historical time' (and not 'structural time') is one of the dimensions of the political field. They suggest, therefore, a 'diachronic method of analysis' linked to an interpretation of political action as 'development' – or a sequence involving differentiated phases (Schwartz, Turner, Tuden, 1966, pp. 8, 31 ff.).

The critical effect is also operating in work of a structuralist orientation; and not only in the sense that it abolishes history, or reduces it to the play of the internal dynamic. This approach is more appropriate to the analysis of ideologies than to the examination of the real political structures to which they are linked. It tries to fix what is essentially dynamic and shows an inadequate grasp of complex and unstable systems of revelations. It is still applied to isolated systems of limited extent – conditions that are the opposite of those required by political anthropology. These remarks have already been made in greater detail. But it should be remembered that structuralism has been unable to offer a solution on the very ground that is, *par excellence*, its own: that of formalization, the elaboration of adequate models, the construction of types. It has not provided political anthropologists with new typologies of a more scientific nature. It has not provided them (and with very good reason) with complex models that would enable them to treat political phenomena in a formal way without either reducing them to other terms or depriving them of their very nature. These phenomena, because of the synthetic or totalizing aspect of their dynamism, present an obstacle to an enterprise of this nature; they cannot be reduced to the formal structures so far used by the social sciences. This fact has led certain political scientists – notably

Almond and Apter – to express the need for different models, for dynamic or 'development' models. This is little more than a vague wish, but it reveals the impossibility of the present situation. The theoretical position of Leach, a moderate structuralist, whose work is partly devoted to the elucidation of traditional political phenomena, is even more significant. It is in *nonpolitical* fields, such as kinship and myth, where the aspect of 'language' is apparent, that Leach emerges fully as a practitioner of the method of structural analysis.

It is unquestionable that political anthropology modifies the perspectives of social anthropology: it is beginning to overthrow the theoretical landscape and transform the familiar configurations. It imposes a more dynamic conception, one more favourable to the consideration of history, more conscious of the strategies which any society (even an archaic one) must bear within itself. In 1957, in a study devoted to the 'factions' operating within Indian societies, Firth announced that it was necessary to pass from 'conventional structural analysis' to research on a rigorous interpretation of 'dynamic phenomena'. Since that date, the decline has continued. In 1955, in my *Sociologie actuelle de l'Afrique noire*, I had already tried to reverse this tendency. But in that work the approach to be followed was suggested rather that made explicit. It was the examination of African political systems that made it necessary to clarify its theoretical and methodological elements – and for the same reasons that have been reiterated in this conclusion: 'the political sector is one of those most marked by history, one of those in which the incompatibilities, contradictions and tensions inherent in any society are best seen at work. For this reason such a level of social reality has a strategic importance for a sociology and an anthropology that wish to be open to history, responsive to the dynamism of the structures and capable of grasping total social phenomena' (Balandier, 1964). The editors and contributors of *Political Anthropology* share this view. They invoke Hegel (and the dialectic), Marx (and the theory of contradiction and antagonisms) and Simmel (and social conflict), though they refer mainly, as usual, to Talcott Parsons. They choose the 'political field' rather than the political system, the process rather than the structure – in order to adjust their analysis to the order of reality under consideration. They reject the facile interpretation that condemns traditional (or archaic) societies to mere repetitive changes: those that culminate in the cyclic re-establishment of the *status quo ante*. Their studies are centred on the dynamic of power, the forms and means of political choice and decision, the expression and resolution of conflict, the struggle and play of factions. They are aware of the importance of the challenge that anthropologists can no longer avoid: to succeed in describing and interpreting the 'social fields', while taking into account 'their full complexity and their temporal depth' (Schwartz, Turner, Tuden, 1966, pp. 3–4). Alibis that distort reality in the interests of rigour are rejected. Political anthropology has at last acquired a corrosive quality.

The other disciplines linked to the construction of political science are still awaiting such a salutary attack. It helps them to *displace* and *test* the knowledge that they have accumulated. A number of convergences emerge: political scientists like Almond recognize that they 'have had to turn to sociological and anthropological theory' (Almond and Coleman, 1960, p. 4), while the political anthropologists are trying to overcome the break that separates them from their 'parents'. This encounter has the effect of questioning commonly held concepts and categories. Thus, M. G. Smith – in a study of the 'government' of the Hausa of Nigeria and its theoretical requirements – attempts to define once again the basic notions of power/ authority, political action/administrative action, legitimacy/ legality, political system/government, etc. He wishes to give them a general significance, to make them applicable to the most varied political societies. At the stage of diachronic analysis he carries this need for generalization to the point at which he claims to have discovered 'laws of structural change'. His highly ambitious enterprise tends towards the development of a unified theory of the political field.

The coalition of these various efforts is in fact a result of the search for suitable conditions for a less arbitrary *comparative* study. For E. Shils, such a study must fulfil at least two requirements: it must use categories that are relevant to all forms of the state, all societies and all periods and must possess an 'analytic scheme' so constituted that different societies may be systematically compared (Shils, 1963). It is an attempt to define methods; nothing more. Almond tries to determine the political systems – including, of course, the most 'primitive' societies – by common characteristics. These are four in number and constitute the poles of a comparison regarded as being scientifically based: the need of a more or less specialized structure; the performance of the same functions within the systems; the multifunctional aspect of the political structure; the 'mixed' character – 'in the cultural sense' – of the various systems. The approach combines several theoretical tendencies and it is vulnerable on account of its syncretism. Above all, it has the inconvenience, at this level of generalization, of being organized on the basis of properties that are not exclusively applicable to political phenomena. There is a constant danger of establishing the comparative analysis on a level at which, though apparently justified, it is deprived of part of its substance. In *Political Anthropology*, Schwartz, Turner and Tuden retain the political field and the political process (qualified by means of concepts in general use) as units of application of comparative research. They prudently confine themselves to suggestions and to the first attempts at verification.

Subsequent progress will require a better knowledge of the nature and essence of the political – and it is this that justifies and necessitates the dialogue between the disciplines concerned. It also requires an end to the suspicion with which political philosophy is commonly held and a contribution to its renewal. Political anthropologists have collaborated widely in the critical work that is dissociating political theory and the theory of the state. They have broken the spell. They have also revealed certain of the by-ways of politics; politics is present in the least organized societies and in situations least favourable to its emergence. All affirmations to the contrary – even when disguised as science – can do nothing to change this. All human societies produce politics and none are resistant to the historical process – for the same reasons.

References

Almond, G. A., and Coleman, J. S. (1960), *The Politics of the Developing Areas*, Princeton University Press, Princeton.

Althabe, G. (1968), *Communautés villageoises de la côte malgache*, Paris.

Ansart, P. (1967), *Sociologie de Proudhon*, Presses Universitaires, Paris.

Apter, D. (1961), *The Political Kingdom in Uganda*, Princeton University Press, Princeton.

Apter, D. (1965), *The Politics of Modernization*, University of Chicago Press, Chicago.

Apthorpe, R. (1960), 'Centralization and role differentiation', *Civilisations*, vol. 10, no. 2.

Aron, R. (1965), 'La sociologie politique', *La Sociologie*, Revue de l'Enseignement Supérieur, Paris.

A.S.A. (1965), *Political Systems and the Distribution of Power*, Monographs 2, London.

Balandier, G. (1962), 'Les mythes politiques de colonisation et de décolonisation en Afrique', *Cah. int. Sociol.*, vol. 33, Paris.

Balandier, G. (1963), *Sociologie actuelle de l'Afrique noire*, Presses Universitaires, Paris.

Balandier, G. (1964), 'Reflexions sur le fait politique: le cas des sociétés africaines', *Cah. int. Sociol.*, vol. 33, Paris.

Balandier, G. (1965a), 'Problématique des classes sociales en Afrique noire', *Cah. int. Sociol.*, vol. 38, Paris.

Balandier, G. (1965b), *La vie quotidienne au royaume de Kongo, du XVIe au XVIIIe siècle*, Hachette, Paris.

Bastide, R. (1965), *Formes élémentaires de la stratification sociale*, C.D.U., Paris.

Beattie, J. H. M. (1959a), 'Checks on the abuse of political power in some African States', *Sociologus*, vol. 9, no. 2.

Beattie, J. H. M. (1959b), 'Rituals of Nyoro kinship', *Africa*, vol. 29, no. 2.

Beattie, J. H. M. (1960a), *Bunyoro, an African Kingdom*, Holt, Rinehart & Winston, New York.

Beattie, J. H. M. (1960b), 'On the Nyoro concept of Mahano', *Afr. Studies*, vol. 19, no. 3.

Beattie, J. H. M. (1964), 'Bunyoro: an African feudality?', *J. Afr. Hist.*, vol. 5, no. 1.

Bergeron, G. (1965), *Fonctionnement de l'état*, Colin, Paris.

Berque, J. (1960), *Les Arabes d'hier à demain*, Éditions du Seuil, Paris.

Bloch, M. (1949), *La société féodale*, Paris.

Bohannan, L. (1958), in J. Middleton and D. Tait (eds.), *Tribes Without Rulers*, Routledge & Kegan Paul, London.

Bohannan, L., and Bohannan, P. (1953), *The Tiv of Central Nigeria*, International African Institute, London.

Busia, K. A. (1951), *The Position of the Chief in the Modern Political System of Ashanti*, Cass, London.

Caillois, R. (1939), *L'homme et le sacré*, Paris.

Calame-Griaule, G. (1966), *Ethnologie et langage, la parole chez les Dogon*, Gallimard, Paris.

Dumézil, G. (1943), *Servius et la fortune*, Nouvelle revue française, Paris.

Dumont, L. (1966), *Homo Hierarchicus, essai sur le système des castes*, Gallimard, Paris.

Durkheim, E. (1893), *De la division du travail social*, Paris.

Durkheim, E. (1950), *Leçons de sociologie*, Introduction by G. Davy, Presses Universitaires, Paris.

Durkheim, E., and Mauss, M. (1901-2), 'De quelques formes de classification', *Année sociol.*, vol. 6, Paris.

Easton, D. (1953), *The Political System*, Knopf, New York.

Easton, D. (1959), 'Political Anthropology', in B. Siegel (ed.), *Biennial Review of Anthropology*, Stanford University Press, Stanford.

Eisenstadt, S. N. (1954), 'African age-groups, a comparative study', *Africa*, April.

Eisenstadt, S. N. (1959), 'Primitive political systems: a preliminary comparative analysis', *Amer. Anthr.*, vol. 61.

Emmet, D. (1958), *Function, Purpose and Powers*, New York.

Evans-Pritchard, E. E. (1940), *The Nuer*, Clarendon Press, London.

Evans-Pritchard, E. E., and Fortes, M. (eds.) (1946), *African Political Systems*, International African Institute, London.

Fallers, L. (1965), *Bantu Bureaucracy*, University of Chicago Press, Chicago.

Favret, J. (1963), 'Le traditionalisme par excès de modernité', *Archiv. europ. Sociol.*, vol. 8, Paris.

Firth, R. (1964), *Essays on Social Organization and Value*, Athlone Press, London.

Fortes, M. (1959), *Oedipus and Job in West African Religion*, Cambridge University Press, Cambridge.

Fortes, M. (1962), 'Ritual and office in tribal society', in M. Gluckman (ed.), *Essays on the Ritual of Social Relations*, Manchester University Press, Manchester.

Freund, J. (1964), *L'essence du politique*, Sirey, Paris.

Freund, J. (1969), *The Sociology of Max Weber*, trans. Anne Carter, Allen Lane The Penguin Press.

Fried, M. H. (1957), 'The classification of corporate unilineal descent groups', *J. roy. Anthr. Instit.*, vol. 87, no. 1, London.

Fried, M. H. (1960), 'The evolution of social stratification and the state', in S. Diamond (ed.), *Culture in History*, Columbia University Press, New York.

Geertz, C. (1963), 'The integrative revolution', in C. Geertz (ed.), *Old Societies and New States*, Free Press, New York.

Gifford, E. W. (1929), *Tongan Society*, Honolulu.

Gluckman, M. (1963), *Order and Rebellion in Tribal Africa*, Cohen, London.

Gluckman, M. (1965), *Politics, Law and Ritual in Tribal Society*, Clarendon Press, London.

Goody, J. (1963), 'Feudalism in Africa?', *J. Afric. Hist.*, vol. 4, no. 1, London.

Guiart, J. (1963), *Structure de la chefferie en Mélanesie du Sud*, Institut d'Ethnologie, Université de Paris.

Gurvitch, G. (1954), *Le concept de classes sociales*, Presses Universitaires, Paris.

Hagen, E. (1964), *On the Theory of Social Change*, London.

Halpern, M. (1963), *The Politics of Social Change in the Middle East and North Africa*, Princeton University Press, Princeton.

Heusch, L. de (1959), *Essais sur le symbolisme de l'inceste royal en Afrique*, Brussels.

Heusch, L. de (1962), 'Pour une dialectique de la sacralité du pouvoir', *Le pouvoir et le sacré*, Annales du Centre d'Étude des Religions, Brussels.

Heusch, L. de (1964), 'Mythe et société féodale', *Arch. Soc. Relig.*, vol. 18.

Heusch, L. de (1966), *Le Rwanda et la civilisation interlacustre*, Institut de Sociologie, Université Libre de Bruxelles.

Hobsbawm, E. J. (1959), *Primitive Rebels*, Manchester University Press, Manchester.

Hsu, F. L. (1963), *Clan, Caste and Club*, Princeton University Press, Princeton.

Ibn Khaldoûn (1965), *Les textes sociologiques et économiques de la Mouquaddima, 1375-9*, G. H. Bousquet (ed.), Paris.

Koppers, W. (1954), 'Remarque sur l'origine de l'état et de la société', *Diogène*, vol. 5.

Koppers, W. (1963), 'L'origine de l'état, un essai de méthodologie', *VIe Congrès int. Sci. anthropol. ethnol.*, t. 2, vol. 1.

Leach, E. (1964), *Political Systems of Highland Burma*; new edn, G. Bell, London.

Leach, E. (1966), 'The legitimacy of Solomon; some structural aspects of Old Testament history', *Archiv. europ. Sociol.*, vol. 7, no. 1.

Leenhardt, M. (1930), *Notes d'ethnologie neo-calédonienne*, Institut d'Ethnologie, Paris.

Lemarchand, R. (1966), 'Power and stratification in Rwanda; a reconsideration', *Cah. d'Études afr.*, vol. 24.

Lewis, H. S. (1966), 'The origins of African kingdoms', *Cah. d'Études afr.*, vol. 23.

Lewis, I. M. (1965), 'Problems in the comparative study of unilineal descent groups', in A.S.A. *The Relevance of Models for Social Anthropology*, London.

Linton, R. (1936), *The Study of Man*, Appleton, New York.

Lloyd, P. C. (1965), *Political Systems and the Distribution of Power*, A.S.A. Symposium, London.

Lowie, R. (1927), *The Origin of the State*, Russell & Russell, New York.

Lowie, R. (1948a), *Social Organization*, Holt, Rinehart & Winston, New York.

Lowie, R. (1948b), 'Some aspects of social organization among the American aborigines', *J. roy Anthr. Instit.*, vol. 78, London.

MacIver, R. (1965), *The Web of Government*, (rev. edn) Free Press, New York.

Macleod, W. C. (1924), *The Origin of the State*, Philadelphia.

Mair, L. P. (1962), *Primitive Government*, Penguin Books, Harmondsworth.

Malinowski, B. (1936), *The Foundations of Faith and Morals*, London.

Malinowski, B. (1947), *Freedom and Civilization*, Allen & Unwin, London.

Maquet, J. (1961), 'Une hypothèse pour l'étude des féodalties africaines', *Cah. d'Études afr.*, vol. 6.

Maquet, J. M. (1964), 'La participation de la classe paysanne au mouvement d'indépendence du Rwanda', *Cah. d'Études afr.*, vol. 16.

Métais, P. (1956), *Mariage et équilibre social dans les sociétés primitives*, Institut d'Ethnologie, Université de Paris.

Métais, P. (1961), 'Problèmes de sociologie néo-calédonienne', *Cah. int. Sociol.*, vol. 30.

Métraux, A. (1962), *Les Incas*, Éditions du Seuil, Paris.

Meyer, E. (1912), *Histoire de l'Antiquité*, Paris.

Middleton, J. (1960), *Lugbara Religion: Ritual and Authority among the East African People*, Holt, Rinehart & Winston, London.

Morgan, L. H. (1964), *Ancient Society*, Oxford University Press, London.

Murdock, G. P. (1834), *Our Primitive Contemporaries*, Macmillan, New York.

Mus, P. (1952), *Viêt-Nam, sociologie d'une guerre*, Éditions du Seuil, Paris.

Myrdal, J. (1964), *Report from a Chinese Village*, Penguin Books, Harmondsworth.

Nadel, S. F. (1942), *A Black Byzantium: The Kingdom of the Nupe of Nigeria*, Oxford University Press for the Institute of African Languages and Culture, Oxford.

Nadel, S. F. (1961), *The Foundation of Social Anthropology*, Cohen, London.

Parkinson, C. N. (1958), *The Evolution of Political Thought*, University of London Press, London.

Perrot, C. H. (1967), '*Be di murua*: un rituel d'inversion sociale dans le royaume agni de l'Indénie', *Cah. d'Études afr.*, vol. 7.

Pocock, D. F. (1961), *Social Anthropology*, Sheed & Ward, London.

Pouillon, J. (1964), 'La structure du pouvoir chez les Hadjerai (Tchad)', *L'Homme*, Sept./Dec.

Richards, A. I. (1960), 'Social Mechanisms for the transfer of political rights in some African tribes', *J. roy. Anthr. Instit.*, vol. 90, no. 2, London.

Rüstow, A. (1950–52), *Ortsbestimmung der Gegenwart*, 2 vols., Zürich.

Sahlins, M. D. (1958), *Social Stratification in Polynesia*, University of Washington Press, Seattle.

Schapera, I. (1956), *Government and Politics in Tribal Societies*, Watts, London.

Schwartz, M., Turner, V., and Tuden, A. (1966), *Political Anthropology*, University of Chicago Press, Chicago.

Shils, E. (1963), 'On the comparative study of the New States', in C. Geertz (ed.), *Old Societies and New States*, Free Press, New York.

Skinner, E. P. (1964), *The Mossi of the Upper Volta*, Stanford University Press, Stanford.

Smith, M. G. (1956), 'On segmentary lineage systems', *J. roy. Anthr. Instit.*, vol. 86, no. 2, London.

Smith, M. G. (1960), *Government of Zazzau, 1800–1950*, Oxford University Press, Oxford.

Southall, A. W. (1956), *Alur Society: A Study in Processes and Types of Domination*, Cambridge University Press, Cambridge.

Sperber, D. (1967), 'Edmund Leach et les anthropologues', *Cah. int. Sociol.*, vol. 43.

Stair, J. B. (1897), *Old Samoa*, Religious Tract Society, London.

Steward, J. H. (1966), in A. L. Kroeber (ed.) *Anthropology Today*, University of Chicago Press, Chicago.

Sutton, F. X. (1959), 'Representation and nature of political systems', *Compar. Studies Sociol. Hist.*, vol. 2, no. 1.

Swanton, J. R. (1911), *Indian Tribes of the Lower Mississippi Valley*, New York.

Teggart, F. J. (1918), *The Processes of History*, Milford, London.

Troubworst, A. (1961), 'L'organisation politique en tant que système d'échange au Burundi', *Anthropologia*, vol. 3, no. 1.

Troubworst, A. (1962), 'L'organisation politique et l'accord de clientèle au Burundi', *Anthropologia*, vol. 4, no. 1.

Van Velsen, J. (1964), *The Politics of Kinship: A Study in Social Manipulation among the Lakeside Tonga of Nyasaland*, Manchester University Press, Manchester.

Vansina, J. (1962), 'A comparison of African kingdoms', *Africa*, vol. 32, no. 4.

Weber, M. (1958), *Gesammelte politische Schriften*, 2nd edn, Tübingen.

White, L. A. (1959), *The Evolution of Culture*, McGraw-Hill, New York.

Williamson, R. W. (1924), *The Social and Political Systems of Central Polynesia*, vol. 1, Humanities Press, New York.

Wilson, M. Hunter (1960), 'Myths of precedence', *Myth in Modern Africa*, Lusaka.

Wittfogel, K. A. (1957), *Oriental Despotism: A Comparative Study of Total Power*, Yale University Press, New Haven.

Select Bibliography

Althusser, L. (1950), *Montesquieu, la politique et l'histoire*, Paris.
Banton, M. (ed.) (1965), *Political Systems and the Distribution of Power*, A.S.A. Monographs 2, London.
Beattie, J. (1964), *Other Cultures, Aims, Methods and Achievements in Social Anthropology*, Routledge & Kegan Paul, London.
Bohannan, L. (1952), 'A genealogical charter', *Africa*, vol. 22, no. 4.
Clastres, P. (1962), 'Échange et pouvoir: philosophie de la chefferie indienne', *L'Homme*, Jan./April.
Cunnison, I. G. (1959), *The Luapula Peoples of Northern Rhodesia: Custom and History in Tribal Politics*, Manchester University Press, Manchester.
Fallers, L. (1965), 'Political anthropology in Africa', in *New Directions in Anthropology*, London.
Firth, R. (1936), *We, The Tikopia*, Allen & Unwin, London.
Fortes, M. (1945), *The Dynamics of Clanship among the Tallensi*, International African Institute, London.
Lewis, I. M. (1961), *A Pastoral Democracy: a Study of Pastoralism and Politics among the Northern Somali*, International African Institute, London.
Radcliffe-Brown, A. R. (1952), *Structure and Function in Primitive Society*, Cohen, London.
Uberoi, J. P. S. (1962), *Politics of the Kula Ring: An Analysis of the Findings of Bronislaw Malinowski*, Manchester University Press, Manchester.

Index of Authors

Index of Subjects